the JUHU BEACH CLUB COOKBOOK

INDIAN SPICE, OAKLAND SOUL

Preeti Mistry with Sarah Henry

Photographs by Alanna Hale

Running Press
PHILADELPHIA

Running Press
Hachette Book Group
1290 Avenue of the Americas, New York, NY 10104
www.runningpress.com
@Running_Press

Printed in China

First Edition: October 2017

Published by Running Press, an imprint of Perseus Books, LLC,
a subsidiary of Hachette Book Group, Inc.

The Hachette Speakers Bureau provides a wide range of authors
for speaking events. To find out more, go to www.hachettespeakersbureau.com
or call (866) 376-6591.

The publisher is not responsible for websites (or their content)
that are not owned by the publisher.

Library of Congress Control Number: 2017945078

ISBNs: 978-0-7624-6245-2 (hardcover)
978-0-7624-6246-9 (ebook)

RRD-S

9 8 7 6 5 4 3 2 1

Archival photographs courtesy of Lisa Bach, the Mistry family,
and Jilchristina Vest.

INTRODUCTION

I thought I was going to start out with a food truck. But back in 2010 Ann, my then-girlfriend and now-wife, kept nudging me to do a pop-up at the slightly sketchy liquor store across the street from our South of Market loft in San Francisco. It's the sort of place you'd drive right by without giving it a thought. The Garage Café, as it's known, was where I went for beer, snacks, scratchers, and emergency milk for the six years we lived in the neighborhood.

It had a kitchen hood, which clears grease, smoke, and heat above a cooktop. That was about all the store had to recommend it. But it was an important detail. You need a hood to deep-fry; you can't cook Indian street food without deep-frying. That's Juhu Beach Club: It's the hot dogs and funnel cakes of Indian cuisine.

Still, I'm a chef who's cooked in fine dining and corporate food service. So the idea of this disorganized, filthy space selling convenience foods . . . my first inclination was to turn my nose up at it. But I didn't. Instead, I approached the owner, he was open to the idea, and we figured out an informal agreement about what hours we could open and what equipment we could use.

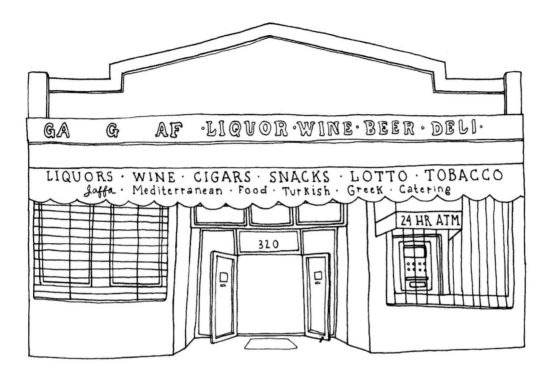

We spent days cleaning. I worked on a menu. We had no idea if people would come. Though not wholly positive, the *Top Chef* TV exposure from the year before helped: Who is this woman and can she cook? People were curious: they came, they ate, they wrote about it.

But the first day, before we opened for business, I was totally scared. I felt a lump in my throat. My mom told me to pray. I don't pray. But the first morning of the pop-up I brought in a small statue of Ganesh and prayed. A friend's son gave me a little green plastic toy for good luck. I kept it in my pocket every day back then.

I felt like this was my one chance. I could not fuck it up.

I made sandwiches, samosas, and a *lassi* to start with. I was doing something different, flavor profile–wise; it wasn't your typical Indian food.

People liked the pop-up. They really liked it. I made just three sandwiches at first: a spicy, veggie sloppy joe; a grilled green chile chicken with tangy turmeric slaw; and a smoky black cardamom braised short rib with a cucumber *raita*. I served them on Acme torpedo buns. They were both familiar fare and a flavor adventure. I sold samosas I rolled by hand and my kind of lassi: a little sweet, a bit salty, the kind an adult would enjoy.

Word started to spread on Twitter and elsewhere in social media. By the

end of six months we were cramming more people into that liquor store than I ever imagined possible, and the menu was a page long. I had developed a loyal following.

Now I needed a place of my own.

I had some false starts. First, I tried to find a home for a restaurant with an investment partner in San Francisco's Mission District. It's a long story: there were permitting issues, budgetary constraints, and contract disputes—too many points of contention. I didn't want to walk away, but I had to. So the deal fell through. It was such a bummer: It was an amazing space, a corner spot with high ceilings. That left me without a financial backer and without a space to call my own in San Francisco.

It happens a lot in this industry. But when it happens to you—out of the blue—it's a major blow. I'd been telling everyone I was about to open a restaurant in the city. Then it became clear that wasn't going to happen. San Francisco is a very expensive place to try to launch a first-time restaurant when you don't have access to a lot of capital.

It felt like another kick in the teeth. I had thought my dreams were going to come true. Everywhere I turned there were roadblocks. I cried.

I'd failed—again. What was I going to do now?

It all ended up working out. Ann and I pooled our savings, and with financial help from my parents, we had enough money to secure a lease on an existing restaurant in Oakland. Juhu Beach Club is now in its fourth year in its humble home in a little strip mall behind a check-cashing outlet and a pawnshop. Ann and I found our home in Oakland as well; it's a good fit for us.

This is my story—failing up and being true to myself—every step of the way. It's Juhu Beach Club's story too: Indian spice and Oakland soul.

HOW TO USE
THIS BOOK

The recipes in this cookbook are arranged in an intentionally eclectic fashion. For instance, recipes aren't listed by the season, menu, dish type, part of the day, ingredients, timeline chronology, or other traditional cookbook conventions.

The recipes are grouped around the stories and anecdotes that precede them and reflect the theme of a chapter, be it street eats, comfort food, Oakland, farm fresh, signature dishes, or so-called authentic cooking. My personal journey and my cooking career, those two things are pretty much tied together these days. It's tough, maybe even impossible, to tease them apart.

There is some logic to this unorthodox approach: All the building-block recipes are in one place, at the beginning of the book. The masalas or spice blends that show up in almost all the recipes in these pages are grouped in one chapter, as are all the restaurant's signature slider sandwiches, known as *pavs*, found on the Juhu Beach Club menu. The chutneys and sauces that are used in multiple recipes are described in full on first usage, then cross-referenced in subsequent recipes, as needed. In general, within a chapter recipes are organized from simple to more complex in nature, and from snacks and starters to main dishes.

Adult beverages seemed to belong in a chapter called Failing Up—cheers to that—so that's where all the drink recipes are housed. Thanks, in advance, for humoring me on that score. Finally, it seemed fitting to end on a sweet note—the one dessert in the book—and a special occasion dish at that.

Trust me, a sense of order will reveal itself to you—especially if you read the material that comes before the recipes. My hope is that something in these pages—whether words, images, or recipes—whets your appetite to pick a dish or two or more to make in your kitchen.

I want to introduce Indian food lovers and adventurous home cooks to the joys of making modern masalas from scratch, along with the popular dishes that have become required ordering at the restaurant. And yes, a recipe for the Manchurian Cauliflower can be found in these pages. So you can surf through this book by recipe—use the recipe list on page 278 or the index on page 279 as a guide, or dip into a chapter that piques your interest and go from there.

As you can see, this cookbook is a reflection of my personality and sensibility.

Here's to failing up in the kitchen. Come join me.

Some of the special ingredients, preferred brands, and specific equipment needed to make the recipes in this book can take a little legwork to find. To begin with, look for an Indian grocery store in your area. Indian grocers have popped up in just about every midsize city in the United States. Aside from remote, rural locations, there is usually an Indian grocery shop within easy driving distance of most Americans. To find an Indian grocery store in the United States near you, hop online and consult this site: thokalath.com/grocery.

The Indian grocery is your first place to go to source spices, produce, lentils, and other ingredients not readily available at conventional supermarkets. That said, many specialty food shops or big supermarkets in large cities may also stock these supplies. Indian shop owners may also be able to help source ingredients or equipment that they don't already have in their inventory. Just ask; they'll likely know where to find an item or can order it for you.

My preferred online resources for sourcing Indian ingredients include Kalustyan's: kalustyans.com; Patel Brothers: patelbrothersusa.com; and World Spice Merchants: worldspice.com.

THE JBC PANTRY: SOURCING SPICES, INGREDIENTS, AND TOOLS

PANTRY STAPLES

Butter

We use a lot of butter at the restaurant, but I'm not attached to a particular brand. We use unsalted butter, always, and I recommend using butter as a substitute for ghee over any other oil.

Chickpeas/Chana

Canned chickpeas are a poor substitute for dried chana that have been soaked for at least six hours and then cooked on the stove. Make a batch, which will keep for up to a week in the fridge, and in addition to the uses in this cookbook, add to salads, stews, soups, dips, or veggie burgers.

Coconut Milk

We prefer the Chaokoh brand. It's the richest coconut milk I've found. It's a welcome addition to curries, and as a bonus it adds a dairy-like creaminess without animal products—which keeps vegans happy.

Dal

Find moong dal, also known as mung beans; toor dal, a bright yellow lentil; and urad dal, a white lentil, in packages or in the bulk aisle at an Indian grocery, specialty market, or online. Buy in the smallest quantities needed to ensure freshness.

Garlic

At the restaurant we use pre-peeled, whole cloves of garlic, due to the high volume we go through. But we don't use pre-minced or puréed garlic, and you shouldn't either. Home cooks can quickly peel a few cloves of garlic as needed, and you'll find this aromatic in most recipes here.

Ghee

A recipe for ghee, also known as clarified butter, is found on page 22. Ghee is made from boiling butter until it becomes clear (or clarified) and browned milk solids settle to the bottom of the pot. Ghee keeps for a long time, so I recommend buying your preferred unsalted butter and making it at home. Store-bought ghee is not very economical, and you can't control the flavor. Besides, you miss out on the rich, nutty fragrance that wafts through the house when you make it.

Ginger

Fresh ginger is a cornerstone of most JBC dishes, including the vast majority of the recipes in this book. It adds so

much pungency and flavor to every recipe it's in. Everyone has a trick for cutting this knobby rhizome: some peel it using the back of a teaspoon; I just use a sharp paring knife. Fresh is best: Those puréed packets of ginger tend to sit, which can lead to an unpleasant bitterness. Simply prep ginger as you go for best results.

Oil

The main fat we use in our restaurant aside from ghee is rice bran oil. Rice bran oil is extracted from the outer brown bran layer of rice, as well as the rice germ, after the husk has been removed. Rice bran oil is excellent for high-heat applications, such as deep-frying or stir-frying, because it has a very high smoke point of 450ºF. It is also totally neutral in color, flavor, and fragrance, making it a versatile oil for a wide range of dishes. If you can't find rice oil, I recommend another neutral oil like sunflower, safflower, or canola oil. In the restaurant our preferred brand is Rito rice bran oil.

Rice

Basmati rice is my rice of choice because it's what I grew up eating and I appreciate the mild, delicate flavor and instantly recognizable aroma of this long grain variety, grown in northern India. Basmati rice is best rinsed in a couple of changes of water to remove any starch, and then soaked for 20 minutes to allow the grains to lengthen, a step that many home cooks miss. This crucial step improves the taste and texture of the rice and reduces the cooking time as the grains soften from soaking. Avoid oversoaking, though, which can cause the grains to break and fall apart during cooking.

Salt

Salt plays a big supporting role in JBC recipes and in this book: It helps bring out the flavors in masalas, marinades, and meats, and enlivens the taste of fruits and vegetables. So taste and season as you cook, and adjust as your palate and dietary restrictions dictate.

Unless otherwise indicated, we use Diamond Crystal Kosher Salt. I recommend it or any other kosher sea salt. In certain recipes, we use a flaky finishing salt on dishes; in those cases, I suggest Maldon Sea Salt. It is readily available at most grocery stores with a broad salt selection.

Tomatoes

In the summertime, when tomatoes are in season, we use either fresh Early Girl or San Marzano tomatoes in our sauces. They offer the best form and flavor for our recipes. The rest of the year we use organic canned whole tomatoes. I recommend paying a little more for organic tomatoes: They really make a difference to the taste and texture of a dish. At the restaurant, we prefer to buy whole canned tomatoes, and then break them down or purée them in dishes, as needed.

Yogurt

Yogurt is a key ingredient on the JBC menu. At the restaurant we use yogurt from Straus Family Creamery, located in nearby Marin County. The quality of their whole plain organic yogurt and Greek-style variety is decadently rich and creamy. If you can't find Straus yogurt near you, use your preferred yogurt brand.

SPECIALTY INGREDIENTS

Chickpea Flour

Chickpea flour, also known as besan flour, gram flour, or garbanzo bean flour, shows up in JBC batters throughout this book. It's a useful alternative to regular flour for gluten-free eaters, and widely available at Indian grocery stores and specialty markets. Chickpea flour adds a slightly nutty flavor to a dish.

Chiles

At JBC our chiles of choice include the dried chile de árbol, for its hot, smoky flavor; the fresh serrano, for its grassy flavor and heat; and the dried ghost pepper, which ranks way up there on the

Scoville scale—that's a measure of the intense pungency of chile peppers found around the world. The ghost pepper chile, also known as *bhut jolokia* in India, is a wrinkly, supercharged spice with a somewhat fruity flavor. We don't deseed our chile peppers: we use it all. The ghost pepper should be handled with caution—wear gloves—and used in moderation, as your taste buds dictate.

Curry Leaves

Fresh curry leaves are essential to many of the dishes in this book. These small, dark green leaves pack a lot of sharp citrus and herby notes when fried alongside other aromatics. There is no real substitute for them. While you may be able to find dried curry leaves, the flavor won't rival their fresh counter-part. Scout your local Indian grocery store to see if it carries fresh curry leaves; if not, ask the grocer to source them for you. Or purchase online. If you like to garden and live in a warm part of the country, you might plant a curry leaf tree in your backyard, that way you'll always have a ready supply and can share or trade with others in the neighborhood. Source seedlings or established trees from a local nursery or online.

Fenugreek Leaves

Fresh fenugreek and curry leaves are generally available in Indian or Chinese grocery stores, or, if you're fortunate, at your local farmers' market. The only substitutes for the fresh leaves, which have a mustardy, musky flavor a little reminiscent of fresh oregano, are frozen or dried fenugreek leaves, which can also be found at Indian grocery stores or purchased online. In this book we use fresh fenugreek leaves in pestos, salsa verdes, and sauces.

Mustard Oil

We use mustard oil in a few different pickles in this book. The oil can be found at most large grocery stores or online. Mustard oil ramps up flavor and adds a thicker viscosity to a pickle brine.

Pavs

Our pavs, or slider-size bread buns, are baked by our friends at Starter Bakery, located just down the street from JBC. If you can't find a bakery close by that makes fresh slider-size buns, you can substitute packaged slider buns from the supermarket. Choose buns that are fluffy and buttery, like a brioche bun.

Tamarind

Look for tamarind blocks at an Indian grocery story. You can buy tamarind pulp (sometimes called concentrate) but making your own is its own reward in terms of the taste payoff. Jarred pastes, pulps, or concentrates lack the fruit's complex flavors, and they aren't cheap. Soak blocks in warm water and remove the flesh from the seeds. This fibrous fruit, with its deeply acidic and tart taste, is used in many dishes in this cookbook.

Turmeric

Due to its newfound popularity in the U.S.—mostly for its antioxidant properties and digestive aid duties—both powdered turmeric and the fresh root are more readily available than ever before. Please be sure to note where

recipes call for the powder or the fresh root of this rhizome, a woody, brown-skinned aromatic that looks a little like ginger but has bright, yellowish-to-orange flesh. It promises a bitter note to dishes and imparts an earthy, mustard-like smell.

Its color is so potent that just a little—less than a teaspoon—is needed to turn a pot of rice a pleasant pale yellow hue, which is how we serve all our rice at JBC.

SPECIALTY SPICES

Whole spices are so central to my cooking that I've devoted an entire chapter to them in this book. For details about common spices, such as cumin seeds, cinnamon sticks, and cardamom pods, see Masala Mash-ups (page 96). Below are notes on less familiar spice friends.

Amchoor

Amchoor (also known as amchur) is dried green mango in powder form, and it adds a welcome sour note to several dishes in this book. Look for it in Indian grocery stores or online. Heads up: A little goes a long way, so you won't need to buy in large quantities.

Black Salt

Kala namak as it is called in Hindi, or Indian black salt, is actually pink when ground. But the Himalayan rocks that it is derived from are black when compacted. Black salt is becoming more widely available; you may be able to find it at a traditional grocery store. Or look for it at an Indian grocery store or online. A word of caution: It has a sulphur smell—much like rotten eggs—so inhale gently when smelling a package of this salt. Rest assured, added in small amounts, it brings a terrific umami dimension to dishes.

Indian Red Chili Powder

Indian red chili powder is much hotter than cayenne, so please do not substitute cayenne pepper. You can find this common, fiery spice in Indian grocery stores or online. Look for a deep red color as an indicator of freshness—the hue fades with time. At JBC we use this powder liberally in sauces, snacks, chutneys, marinades, raitas, and even on the rims of drinks.

A NOTE ON SPICE STORAGE

Store spices in a cool, dry area in jars with tight-fitting lids. Air and light are spices' biggest enemy, and will age and dull them quickly. Don't store spices in the fridge or freezer, this will also dull their flavor and the spices can take on some of the other odors in your fridge or freezer, much like baking soda does. I recommend using whole spices within six months of purchase. Buy spices in quantities that make sense for your home use. Ground spices and blends are most potent if used within two weeks.

TOOLS

Belan

This is a tiny, affordable rolling pin used for rolling out puri dough. Find it in an Indian grocery store or online. A small regular rolling pin will suffice as a substitute, if necessary.

Blenders

We use an immersion blender a ton at the restaurant to purée soups and sauces. An immersion blender, which doesn't take up a lot of room in your kitchen cabinet or cost a lot, allows you to more easily control the texture of a final dish—whether you're looking for a smooth or chunky finish. My preferred tabletop blender is the Vitamix; it's powerful enough for the biggest jobs at the restaurant. But a standard, inexpensive blender for making sauces from this book will do the job.

Food Mill

A food mill is a useful tool that you can find in most kitchen supply stores or online. It is particularly helpful in cooking from this book for puréeing tamarind and mashing potatoes. If you do not have one, you can use a sieve to remove seeds from tamarind, and a potato ricer or masher for the potatoes. In the restaurant we use a pricey one for large batches, but home cooks don't need to fork out for such costly equipment.

Oil & Candy Thermometer

A candy/deep-frying thermometer (the same thermometer works for both purposes) costs about $10 to $15 and can be purchased at kitchen supply stores or online. The thermometer will be invaluable in cooking sugar at the exact temperature required. It will also make sure your oil is at the correct temperature for deep-frying on the stovetop.

Mandoline

We use a mandoline slicer for a number of recipes in this book. There are stainless steel mandolines that can cost upwards of $150, and they will most likely last you a lifetime. If you don't want to make that kind of investment, there are cheaper plastic options that start as low as $15. Just know you will have to replace a plastic mandoline after a certain amount of wear and tear.

Sev Sancho

A *sancho* is a unique Indian kitchen tool, not dissimilar from a Playdoh extruder. We use a sancho when making batter for *sev*, the crispy noodles that garnish several of our dishes. You can buy one either at an Indian grocery store or online. The best sanchos are made from brass—they last longer and are less likely to break—but you can find them in less expensive stainless steel and aluminum as well.

Spice Grinder

An inexpensive electric coffee grinder is the most economical and effective spice grinder for home use. You can buy one in just about any kitchenware store or online. I recommend designating one coffee grinder for spices only. It just makes sense to keep your coffee and spices separate. But if you are in a pinch and need to use your daily grinder to make a masala, the best way to remove any excess grounds from the equipment is to pulse the grinder with a few small pieces of white bread. The bread will pick up the majority of the grounds or spices.

Grind spices only as you need them for the best flavor results. Grinding helps to release the essential oils that make spices such an integral part of Indian cooking. A mortar and pestle can come in handy to crack hard spices such as cinnamon sticks or cardamom pods before grinding, but a spice grinder results in a fine, even spice powder, which is what we're looking for in our masalas.

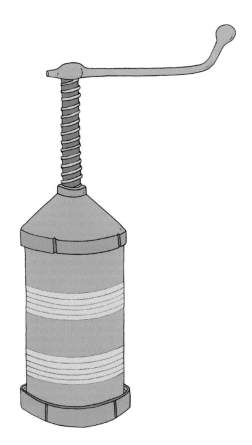

GHEE

Makes 1 quart

2 pounds unsalted butter

I have made ghee for as long as I can remember, but it wasn't until about ten years ago that I mastered my mother's technique quite by accident. Ghee is simply clarified butter—it's what's left when the milk solids separate from the fat. Ghee is a foundation ingredient in Indian cuisine; its comforting, familiar smell permeates Indian kitchens around the globe. Ghee adds a delicious richness to any dish. And yet for many years while my ghee was good, it always seemed to be missing a little something compared to my mom's. My mother is notorious for leaving out ingredients or steps when sharing recipes with others—she's not secretive; there's just this assumed knowledge she forgets to pass on. I discovered that was the case with ghee, when one day I was making it on the stovetop and forgot about it. When I finally remembered to check the pan, I found browned milk solids on the bottom and the most intoxicating aroma. It smelled just like my mother's ghee: clear fat with all the nuttiness of browned butter.

Place the unsalted butter in a heavy-bottom saucepan on medium-low heat. After the butter melts, keep a close eye on it, as liquefied butter may overflow if the temperature gets too high. If the butter looks like it might overflow, remove it from the heat for 10 minutes and then return. Continue cooking on low for about 1 hour. The milk will foam and rise, forming a white film.

After about 30 to 40 minutes the milk solids will start to drop to the bottom of the pan, and a clear clarified butter is left on top. Pay attention to the bottom of the pot now as the milk solids will slowly begin to brown. When all the milk solids have sunk to the bottom and turned golden brown, remove the pan from the heat and strain the ghee with a fine-mesh sieve. Store in a jar in the refrigerator for up to 4 weeks.

TAMARIND PASTE

Makes 1 quart

2 tamarind blocks

Many stores sell puréed tamarind paste. I recommend making it: the flavor is so much better, it is way cheaper, and it keeps in the fridge for one week or in the freezer for up to three months. As a child I remember being confused by ice trays full of brown ice cubes. My mother stored her tamarind that way so she could just pop out one or two cubes at a time, as needed. I follow that practice now, too. This is a good recipe to use a food mill, if you happen to have one.

Place the tamarind blocks in a medium saucepan with 4 cups of water. Make sure the water covers the blocks fully. Bring the water to a boil and simmer for about 15 to 20 minutes on low heat, until the tamarind blocks begin to break down and soften; use a spoon to aid this process. Strain the mixture into a sieve and press with a spoon to extract the pulp, leaving the seeds behind. Alternatively, place the mixture in a food mill and hand crank to create the paste. Store the tamarind paste in an airtight container in the refrigerator for 1 week; for longer storage, transfer to the freezer for up to 3 months.

TOASTED CUMIN

Makes 6 cups

1 cup cumin seeds

This basic ingredient is so common in JBC's cuisine that it's practically the ground pepper equivalent for our menu.

Place the cumin seeds on a sheet pan. Cook in a 350°F oven for 5 to 7 minutes—until the cumin begins to slightly smoke and turn a little brown. Remove the pan from the oven and set it aside to cool. When the seeds are completely cooled, grind them in a spice grinder in batches, until all the cumin is fully ground. Mix well and keep in an airtight container for up to 4 weeks in a cool, dry place.

DATE PASTE

Makes 3 cups

2 cups Medjool dates, pitted

Dates are a natural sweetener in many sauces and desserts. We primarily use this date paste to make tamarind-based sauces; the paste serves as the sweet foil to the tamarind's sourness. The rich depth of a date can't be matched by the quick fixes used in some kitchens—namely sugar or honey.

Place the dates in a medium saucepan with 2 cups of water. Make sure the water covers the dates fully. Bring the water to a boil and simmer for about 5 to 10 minutes on low heat, until the dates begin to break down and soften.

Ladle the dates and water into a blender or food processor. Purée into a thick creamy pulp. Store the date paste in an airtight container in the refrigerator for 1 week; for longer storage transfer to the freezer for up to 3 months.

CITRUS PICKLED ONIONS

Makes 1 quart

3 large red onions, julienned

2 lemons, juiced

2 limes, juiced

1 tablespoon salt

2 tablespoons black salt
(kala namak, as it's called in
Indian grocery stores)

These pickled onions are used in a variety of JBC starters, as well as for toppings on our pavs. This is a quick pickle of red onions and lemon and lime juices with the addition of black salt, which gives them a classic Indian street food flavor and fragrance. Himalayan black salt, or kala namak, is a pungent, sulfuric volcanic salt. In large amounts it smells like rotten eggs. The rock salt itself is black, but when ground, it turns into a pink powder. This pink powder is used in drinks, sauces, and sometimes just liberally sprinkled on top of a dish as a seasoning or condiment. The funky umami taste and aroma are a distinctive addition to street food fare.

Toss the onions with the citrus juices and salts. Set aside in a sealed plastic container in the refrigerator for at least 6 hours. Shake the container every couple of hours to keep juice well distributed throughout the mix. The onions will turn bright red and taste slightly milder than raw, unpickled onions. Keep them refrigerated in an airtight container for up to 1 month.

PRESERVED MEYER LEMONS

Makes 2 quarts

6 pounds Meyer lemons
½ cup salt
¼ cup Dhanna Jeeru Masala
  (see recipe page 102)
2 tablespoons Indian red chili powder
½ cup neutral oil

We have never purchased a Meyer lemon at JBC. I'm not bragging here; it's just the embarrassment of riches that is Northern California backyard bounty. Regular customers and neighbors bring us bags of their surplus lemons constantly. We gladly accept them and make these piquant pickles. They can be used in a number of ways to enhance a sauce, salad, or marinade.

Scrub the lemons vigorously to remove any excess dirt. Juice ⅓ of the lemons, and set the juice aside. Cut the remaining lemons into quarters and toss them with the salt, masala, and chili powder. Pack the seasoned lemons into clean half-gallon glass jars. Pour the lemon juice over the lemons and top with the oil. If the lemons are not fully submerged in liquid, add a bit more oil to cover. Wipe the mouth of each jar and close the lid. Leave the jars out in a cool dry place at room temperature for 2 weeks, shaking them once a day. After 2 weeks, move the jars to the refrigerator; the preserved lemons will keep for up to 6 months.

Chapter One

STREET EATS

'm four years old, in a rickshaw stuck in a traffic jam on my way to Juhu Beach in Mumbai. This is my first trip to India to visit my mother's family. I don't know what to expect from the people or the place. Something appealing captures my attention, and I blurt out: "What's that smell?" The aroma of roasting peanuts fills my nostrils. I want to follow that scent.

We get closer to the source. Finally, I see a sprawling, crescent-shaped expanse of sand overlooking the Arabian Sea. But before you make it to the beach, you wind your way there along Juhu Tara Road—that's the main drag. And there's that sensory hit, a whiff of what lies ahead. It's a mixture of the sea, smoke from coal-fire cooking, and traffic pollution, all melding with the intoxicating scent of roasting peanuts and deep-fried *pakoras* (chickpea batter fritters studded with vegetables).

That's what I recall most about my first trip to Juhu Beach: The food. It's everywhere.

I go back when I'm fifteen. The memories are more vivid. Juhu at dusk, a carnival-like energy. Wherever you look there are people—almost all men—cooking. Parts of the beach are cordoned off and lined with fancy private hotels; other sections resemble a homeless encampment. But big strips of sand are filled with regular folks hanging out with family and friends. Juhu Beach is not a place where people go to swim and lie in the sun during the day; it's too hot. It's the hazy sunset that draws a throng. And it's a magnet for street food lovers.

Juhu Beach is a crowded, chaotic, noisy, hot, colorful, sweaty crush of humanity fed by hawkers peddling snacks: savory dishes such as *puris*, pavs, and *dosas* (a pancake made with fermented batter), and sweet treats like lassi, *gola* (crushed ice on a stick doused in neon-hued flavorings), and *kulfi* (Indian ice cream).

I'm back again at age thirty-four. India and I have a complicated relationship; I needed some distance. This time, though, Juhu Beach and its street food comes home with me. I'll get to that in a second.

⁗⁗⁗⁗⁗⁗⁗⁗⁗

The snacks at this seaside destination—like *pav bhaji*, samosas, *batata vada*, *idlis*, and dosas—are all in my mother's arsenal, but she only makes them for parties and other special occasions. It's not often enough for my taste buds. Growing up in suburban Ohio, we ate healthy, home-cooked Indian fare. Dal-*bhat-rotli-shaak*—that's what we dubbed my mom's daily repertoire. It was basically soup, rice, flatbread, and a dry vegetable sauté. I wasn't a huge fan. I got bored.

I wanted "outside" food. Any food from outside our kitchen felt cosmopolitan and exciting. Jerry Seinfeld eating a hot dog on the streets of Manhattan: I wanted to be a part of that. On occasional visits to Detroit, Chicago, and the Indian mecca that is Edison, New Jersey, I got to indulge my cravings. I wanted more.

||||||||||||||||||||||||

I was born in London. My family entered the United States in Miami, as we had family in Orlando. I was five. My dad was a medical intern trying to get a residency gig. We moved to Pennsylvania to follow his job. In the mid-1980s, when I was ten, we moved again because he joined an anesthesia practice where there was the opportunity to become a partner. Our new home: Ohio. Toledo. Suburbia.

No matter where I lived, I definitely always felt different.

I had this short, little-boy cut. I used to go to the hair salon and ask the stylist to "cut my hair like my dad's." I wore little-boy clothes or at least the most boyish girl's clothes my parents would allow me to have. On special occasions I was forced to wear dresses. I protested loudly; it was never fun for anyone.

From the time I turned four, I said adamantly: "I'm a boy, call me a boy." And then soon after that—I think when we moved to the States—I became aware that that was not okay to say. People didn't want to hear it. It made adults uncomfortable. When it was time for me to get a bike, I wanted a BMX dirt bike, and my parents said: "no, they are for boys."

In Toledo I was brown and boyish. Double whammy.

||||||||||||||||||||||||

Eventually, I fled the suburbs for cities. Two decades pass—I spent them living in urban hubs like London and San Francisco. I avoided India, feeling like I couldn't be my real self there.

That brings us to 2010. In love with my soon-to-be wife Ann, I return to India. We join my parents, who are visiting family and attending a wedding near Mumbai. I have just quit working as a top chef at Google headquarters in the heart of Silicon Valley and am toying with doing an Indian-influenced pop-up in San Francisco. I've already come up with a name for my pop-up: Juhu Beach Club. And I have a sense of what I want to do: seasonal Northern California ingredients infused with the spices and flavors of the Indian street food I love.

On this visit, I go deep on the food front. This isn't just a chance to see extended family and vacation with my mom and dad. This is a research trip. I sample everything. We stay for almost three weeks. We eat a *lot*.

My mother grew up in Mumbai, so she knows where to go. Mumbai is a city for Indians, and Juhu Beach is a destination for Indian tourists. It's not that easy to navigate if you don't speak Hindi, don't know where you're going, or don't know where to eat. My mom falls right back into it and isn't fazed by the intensity, the crazy bumper-to-bumper traffic, the overwhelming crowds. (On the car ride from the airport when I was fifteen, I cried; I had never witnessed poverty like that. I begged my mom to give me some rupees to hand out to people who asked for money. They were hungry. We drove past piles of rubbish and shanty-towns where people lived in the streets alongside chickens. We were not in Ohio anymore.)

So on my visit in my early thirties, I let my mom lead. We have to make one stop before lunch, mom says the first day we're there. She doesn't elaborate. We go with the flow. We pull up next to a dude selling coconuts; he's holding a machete. He hacks the top off each coconut, pops in a straw, and passes them over to us to drink. It's a sweet, fresh flavor jolt, the viscous fluid slides luxuriously down the throat. Then mom asks if we want the jelly—there's this gelatinous layer inside young coconuts before the flesh fully hardens. Of course, we say yes, and pass our coconuts back to the guy, who cuts them down farther. He also takes a little piece of the outer rind and shapes it into a small spoon so we can scoop up the jelly. It dissolves deliciously in our mouths. And then off we go in search of lunch.

I learn how to order *pani puri* on this trip. It's kind of like bellying up to an oyster bar. There's the puri maker at his stand, putting on a performance for the group that's gathered around. I've eaten so many different kinds of street food in India, but pani puri might be my all-time favorite. It's a small pastry puff that's deep-fried into a hollow shell. The street vendor fills it with a mixture of potatoes, chickpeas, and a little bit of raw onion; that's the puri. The pani is a spiced water: tamarind, mint, jaggery (traditional cane sugar), and whatever the seller's *chaat masala* or special blend of dried spices is. You pop the whole thing in your mouth—that's key—only rookies attempt to take a bite. You're rewarded by this burst of flavor: refreshing and spicy all at once. It's like a little *amuse-bouche*: designed to whet the appetite for more.

You want more. Pani puri are made to order, right there, on the spot. The vendor pokes a hole in the crispy sphere with his thumb and passes you another one. He remembers exactly how many you've had when you're finished, whether it's two or twenty. Insider tip: Unless you have a steel stomach, the place to go near Juhu Beach for pani puri is the Elco Pani Puri Centre, where they use bottled water. I learned that from my mom, too.

Rewinding to that trip when I was a teenager—a pouty Midwestern brat sporting an oversize alternative rock band T-shirt and baggy shorts, I travel with my mom and my sister in the ladies' compartment of a train going from Mumbai to Amdavad, also known as Ahmedabad. It's the capital of Gujarat, the western Indian state, where some of my mom's family still live and where my mother spent summers in her childhood.

The train is smelly and crowded. I'm out of my comfort zone and make my displeasure known.

Eventually we find seats. Within an hour or so I go from having my nose turned up to falling asleep on the shoulder of the stranger sitting next to me. I wake up to discover a man moving through the compartment with hot, steaming lentil cakes known as idlis. The aroma of this savory snack accompanied by the swipe of coconut chutney draws me in. I have to have one.

The idli is basically a thicker dosa batter, made with fermented lentils and rice, which give them an appealing, slightly funky smell and flavor, not unlike sourdough bread. They're shaped like a little football. I grew up eating idlis with a bowl of *sambar* or fiery lentil soup; you eat them together, like a giant matzo ball soup. On the train the idlis come without the sambar. It doesn't matter. The pillowy texture of those train vendor idlis pairs perfectly with the tangy hit of chutney. They are the best idlis I've ever had: soft, warm, soothing. Something about eating on the go, surrounded by people, makes this snack extra special. I'd been uncomfortable, hungry, and sweaty and then those idlis showed up, calling my name.

That's the allure of street food. It pops up as you move through a city; it's fleeting—whether it's a hot dog stand in New York City or jacket potatoes in the markets in London or idlis on a long train ride in India. In its purist form, street food doesn't bow to convention: there are no operating hours or taking reservations. There aren't any tables or even menus. Street food vendors just set up shop and sell until they run out or feel like packing up or get summoned home. The spontaneity adds to the excitement of eating. As a teenager, I saw street food as a thing that people in big cities ate, and that is where I knew I belonged.

DESI JACKS

Makes 6 quarts

1 cup pistachios
    (can substitute almonds or
    hazelnuts if needed)
4 cups peanuts
¼ cup neutral oil
    (we use Rito Rice Bran Oil)
1 tablespoon Toasted Cumin
    (see recipe page 25)
1 tablespoon Indian red chili powder
2 tablespoons salt (we use
    Diamond Crystal Kosher)
4 quarts cooked popcorn
¼ cup Ghee (clarified butter)
    (see recipe, page 22) or
    substitute melted butter
2 cups packed light brown sugar
2 cups light corn syrup
2 tablespoons sea salt
    (we use Maldon)

There's nothing traditionally Indian about these popcorn-peanut-pistachio snacks. I just love popcorn and wanted to make a grown-up snack that was sweet, salty, and spicy, an Indian-flavored riff on Cracker Jacks. I recommend using an air popper: It yields better results with less risk of burning the popcorn. Other equipment to have on hand: 2 Silpat mats and a sugar thermometer.

Preheat oven to 350°F. Toss both the nuts with oil, half the cumin, and half the chili powder. Season to taste with salt. Spread onto a sheet pan and roast for 10 to 15 minutes in the oven until golden brown. Let cool, about 10 to 15 minutes.

Season the popcorn with ghee, the rest of the cumin, chili powder, and salt to taste. Toss well to coat evenly. Set aside. Heat the sugar and corn syrup in a large saucepan on high heat. Cook the sugar stirring with a thermometer every few minutes. When the sugar reaches hardball stage (250 to 260°F), add the nuts and popcorn and fold into the caramel. Place the saucepan into the oven for 10 minutes.

Remove it from the oven and stir further if necessary to incorporate the caramel—use caution, as the sugar will be very hot.

Use a large spoon to spread the popcorn caramel mixture onto Silpat mats; flatten out the mixture with the back of the spoon. Sprinkle the mixture with sea salt and let it cool. When it is cool to the touch, break the clumps apart into bite-size pieces. Desi Jacks will keep in an airtight container for 3 to 6 days.

ROASTED GARAM MASALA PEANUTS

Makes 2 quarts

2 eggs, whites only
2 quarts raw peanuts
2 tablespoons JBC Garam Masala
   (see recipe page 103)
2 teaspoons salt

This little snack packs a lot of flavor. When I was a kid, my dad used to offer friends who came to visit roasted peanuts along with a beer or Scotch whisky. Dad served store-bought nuts that he doctored with chili powder and lime. As a little girl I remember feeling that these peanuts were a forbidden pleasure, the stuff of grown men's business. I wanted in on the secret. That longing to be part of the club proved the impetus for creating this spicy and salty snack.

Preheat oven to 350°F. In a medium bowl, whisk the egg whites until frothy but not stiff. Add the nuts and mix well. In another bowl mix together the garam masala and salt. Toss the nuts with the masala and salt. Spread the seasoned nuts onto a baking sheet and roast for about 10 minutes. Reduce the heat to 300°F and roast the peanuts for another 5 to 10 minutes. When the nuts are lightly browned and dry, remove them from the heat and let them cool. Store in an airtight container for one week.

POTATO CHIPS WITH CHAAT MASALA

Makes 6 quarts

2 large russet potatoes
4 quarts neutral oil (for deep-frying)
2 tablespoons salt
½ cup Chaat Masala
   (see recipe page 106)

These chips originally started as a kitchen treat I'd whip up for the Juhu Beach Club cooks. We soon began offering these crunchy bites as a bar snack, and they proved quite the hit. The key is to slice the potatoes superthin—a mandoline is the tool of choice here—to get both the crisp texture of a chip combined with the zesty flavor of the street food spice blend known as chaat masala.

Scrub the potatoes well. Use a mandoline to thinly slice rounds of potato into a bowl of cold water. Rinse the potatoes in a colander to remove the excess starch.

Heat the oil in a large pot—suitable for deep-frying—to 300°F. Use a thermometer to check the temperature. Slowly drop a few potato slices into the hot oil, moving them around to make sure they don't stick to each other. The slices will take 3 to 5 minutes to cook. Test for doneness by tasting to see if the potatoes are crispy all the way through.

When the potato slices are completely crispy, drain them onto a sheet pan lined with paper towels to soak up any excess grease. Sprinkle with the salt and chaat masala.

Continue in batches until all the potatoes are fried. The cooled potato chips keep in an airtight container for 3 days.

PAVS TO THE PEOPLE

Indians love their breads. I grew up with chewy flatbread rotis (whole wheat), and most Americans know the leavened, airy, oven-baked naan. At Juhu Beach, the pav is the preferred bread of choice.

Pavs aren't that well known in the United States. I'm on a mission to change that.

The word *pav* comes from the Portuguese word for bread, which is *pao*. Prior to the arrival of the Portuguese, India was the land of unleavened breads, like roti and chapati. The pav bhaji was likely invented in the 1850s by street food vendors in Mumbai (formerly Bombay), for textile mill workers who needed a fast, cheap, satisfying, but not sleep-inducing lunch. The vendors used leftover veggies as filling, typically tomatoes, carrots, cauliflower, and peas; *bhaji* means vegetables in Marathi, an Indian language spoken in Mumbai.

At Juhu Beach, the bhaji is made on a huge flat griddle called a *tava*. The rolls are so covered in butter they're practically yellow. The bhaji is typically dished up with a generous knob of butter on top, too. It comes on a metal tray with compartments that house a side of raw onion and fresh lime wedges. Customers hungrily mop up the mashed vegetable and masala mix with the buns. It's a sloppy, messy, fiery taste sensation.

I took the concept of the pav, which I grew up eating occasionally from prepackaged spices, and made it my own. I began making it from scratch using whole spices in my twenties. Trust me, you can taste the difference. I want Indian Americans to be surprised by our pulled pork or lamb meatball pavs, and I want Americans who have never heard of a pav to try one. There's more to Indian food than just naan and curry. The Juhu Beach Club version of bhaji—we call it the Sloppy Lil' P—isn't runny; it's shaped into a dome and served on the bun instead of with the bread on the side.

Oh, and about those buns: Typical street food pavs are mass-produced rolls filled with additives and preservatives—but not at Juhu Beach Club. My buddy Brian Wood at Starter Bakery makes pavs especially for the restaurant. Brian's buttery buns are the bomb, almost like brioche.

The pav is the Desi equivalent of an American slider. (Desi used to be a negative term used by people of Indian descent to describe other Indians. In the last decade or two, it's been taken back and is now used in a positive, inclusive way.) We don't hold back on the heat at Juhu Beach Club, hence the lightning bolts on our menu. The pav is no exception.

We pack a lot of tastes and textures into that little slider: sweet, salty, spicy, tangy, bitter, buttery, crunchy, and soft. To me, when all those things come together in one mouthful, it's the essence of what Indian street food is all about.

PULLED PORK VINDALOO PAV

Makes 20 to 24 pavs

For the pulled pork:
2 pounds boneless pork shoulder
1 quart Vindaloo Marinade
  (recipe follows, see page 42)
1 yellow onion, julienned
1 cup canned puréed tomatoes
¼ cup tomato paste
½ cup light brown sugar

For the cilantro slaw:
½ head green cabbage, julienned
2 large carrots, julienned or grated
1 bunch of cilantro, roughly chopped
2 teaspoons Dhanna Jeeru
  Masala (see recipe page 102)
1 teaspoon salt
1 cup whole plain yogurt
  (we use Straus)

2 dozen pavs/slider buns

I enjoy a big, sloppy, meaty sandwich. Inspiration for this pav comes both from Southern-style pulled pork barbecue—that American classic with its signature sweetness—and a traditional Indian dish, pork vindaloo, which promises a spicy tang. We marinate the pork shoulder in fresh curry leaves, chiles, and a spicy vinegar for at least six hours. This sandwich practically demands to be served with a healthy heaping of Cilantro Slaw, recipe follows.

We use pavs—small slider buns made just for JBC by a local baker. Any small slider bun will work here.

Trim any excess fat from the pork and cut it into 4 equal pieces. Pour the marinade over the pork and marinate for at least 6 hours, ideally overnight.

Preheat the oven to 300°F. Transfer the pork and marinade into a heavy-bottom, oven-safe casserole and place on the stovetop to bring to a boil. Add the onion and tomatoes. Cover with a tight-fitting lid or aluminum foil, and place in the oven for 3½ to 4 hours. After 3½ hours, check the pork with tongs. When the meat falls away easily, remove it from the oven and let cool.

Once the pork has cooled enough to handle—about a half hour—remove the meat from the braising liquid and shred it by hand or with tongs and a fork.

(recipe continues)

To make vindaloo barbecue sauce:
Pour the braising liquid into a medium saucepan and place on medium heat. Mix in the tomato paste and brown sugar and cook until fully dissolved—about 10 to 15 minutes—until the sauce is thick. Season with salt as needed.

To make the cilantro slaw:
Toss the cabbage, carrots, cilantro, dhanna jeeru masala, salt, and yogurt together. Mix well and taste. Add more salt as needed.

To assemble the pavs:
Heat the pork with the barbecue sauce until hot, pile onto toasted buns, and top with cilantro slaw.

Vindaloo Marinade

Makes 2 quarts

2 cups fresh curry leaves
1 cup dried red chile de árbol
1 tablespoon ginger
1 tablespoon garlic cloves
1 teaspoon cumin seeds
4 cups white wine vinegar
1 tablespoon kosher salt

Place all the ingredients in a blender and purée until the curry leaves and chiles are completely ground and no whole pieces are left.

BOMBAY-STYLE CURRIED EGG SALAD PAV

Makes 20 to 24 pavs

1 dozen eggs
½ cup whole plain yogurt
   (we use Straus)
2 tablespoons Curry Powder
   (see recipe page 110)
1 tablespoon salt
1 cup roughly chopped cilantro
20 pavs/slider buns
½ English cucumber,
   thinly sliced
2 cups watercress, washed

I grew up eating egg salad sandwiches as a young child living in London. In the JBC version we make our own in-house curry powder. It's similar to the Madras curry powder many people associate with Indian food. But there's a world of difference in the taste of our freshly ground masala compared with store-bought varieties. Just saying.

We use pavs—small slider buns made just for JBC by a local baker. Any small slider bun will work here.

Set the eggs in a large saucepan filled with cold water to cover. Place on high heat. When the water comes to a boil, lower the heat to medium high; the water should be lightly simmering. Set a timer for 8 minutes. After 8 minutes, drain the eggs and run cold water over them. Set the eggs into ice-cold water to fully cool, about 10 minutes. Peel the eggs. Use the largest-size holes on a box grater to grate the eggs into a bowl. Mix in the yogurt, curry powder, salt, and cilantro. Season with salt to taste.

To assemble pavs:
Toast the pavs until lightly browned on a grill or in a broiler. Layer the bottom of each pav with 2 to 3 slices of English cucumber, top with a scoop of egg salad, and garnish with watercress.

CHOWPATTY CHICKEN PAV

Makes 16 to 20 pavs

4 pounds boneless skinless
   chicken thighs

**For the green chile turmeric
   marinade:**
½ cup garlic, peeled
½ cup ginger, peeled
½ cup fresh turmeric root, scrubbed
¼ cup serrano chiles
4 bunches cilantro
1 tablespoon Mustard Fenugreek
   Masala (see recipe page 102)
2 tablespoons salt

For the tangy turmeric slaw:
¼ cup neutral oil
¼ cup fresh curry leaves
1 teaspoon brown mustard seeds
2 jumbo carrots, julienned or grated
½ head green cabbage, julienned
2 teaspoons salt
1 teaspoon turmeric powder
1 teaspoon Indian red chili powder
1 tablespoon white wine vinegar
¼ cup whole plain yogurt

¼ cup neutral oil (for grilling)
20 pavs/slider buns
1 cup Cilantro Chutney
   (recipe follows, see page 46)

The marinade for this chicken pav uses fresh turmeric root, which gives the meat an intense yellow hue. Turmeric root—available at Asian markets and natural foods stores—is known for its health benefits and enjoying a surge in popularity in certain circles, which I find amusing. The marinade for this dish is also excellent on whole pieces of grilled chicken or grilled vegetables. Marinating for at least six hours yields the most flavorful meat. The slaw on this pav is a cold variation of a hot cabbage dish my mother made frequently for dinner. It hits all the right taste notes: crunchy, tangy, and satisfying.

We use pavs—small slider buns made just for JBC by a local baker. Any small slider bun will work here.

Roughly chop the garlic, ginger, fresh turmeric, chiles, and cilantro. Place all the chopped ingredients in a blender. Add ½ cup water, mustard fenugreek masala, and salt. Purée until the mixture has a chunky, pesto-like consistency. If the marinade is too thick, add a ¼ cup more water to the purée. Coat the chicken thighs in the marinade and chill for at least 6 hours or ideally overnight.

To make the slaw:
Heat the oil on high in a large sauté pan or wok. When the oil is just about to smoke, add the curry leaves and mustard seeds. Shake the pan; the ingredients will sizzle and pop. After 1 minute, add the carrot and cabbage and stir to mix the ingredients. Season this cabbage-carrot mixture with salt, turmeric, and chili powder. Stir until the cabbage wilts slightly—about 3 minutes. Then add the vinegar and remove from heat. Let it fully cool—at least 20 minutes—and then fold in the yogurt. Chill in the refrigerator in an airtight container. The slaw will keep for three days.

(recipe continues)

To assemble the pavs:

Heat a grill or broiler to medium-high heat. Toss the chicken thighs with the ¼ cup oil and grill on each side for about 7 minutes until fully cooked. Toast the pavs until lightly browned. Cut the chicken to fit on a toasted pav and top with the cilantro chutney and turmeric slaw.

Cilantro Chutney

Makes 2 cups

1 lemon, juiced
¼ cup ginger
1 tablespoon serrano chiles
⅓ cup whole plain yogurt
2 cups packed, roughly chopped
   cilantro
2 teaspoons salt

In a blender combine lemon juice, ginger, chile, and yogurt. Purée until ginger and chiles are fully integrated into a thick paste. Add the cilantro, using a rubber spatula to submerge the leaves into the purée. Blend again. Stop the blender and push the cilantro down a second time, if needed, to fully purée the ingredients. Season with salt.

SLOPPY LIL' P PAV

Makes 24 to 30 pavs

4 to 6 Yukon Gold potatoes

1 large head cauliflower, trimmed

2 large carrots, peeled

½ pound unsalted butter

2 yellow onions, julienned

¼ cup ginger, minced

¼ cup garlic, minced

¼ cup serrano chile, minced

½ cup Sloppy P Masala
  (see recipe page 104)

2 cups tomato paste

½ pound frozen peas, defrosted

salt, for seasoning

2 teaspoons Tamarind Paste
  (see recipe page 23)

Citrus Pickled Onions (see recipe
  page 26)

24 to 30 pavs/slider buns

Pav bhaji is a popular street food snack all over India, but especially in Gujarat, the state on the country's western coast where my mother's family comes from. Pav bhaji is essentially a fiery, buttery, and onion-laden veggie version of a sloppy joe served with the pavs on the side. My take is a little less runny than its Indian street cart counterpart. Gujarati hawkers typically serve this snack with a wedge of lime. At Juhu Beach Club we top the Sloppy Lil' P Pav with our Citrus Pickled Onions.

We use pavs—small slider buns made just for JBC by a local baker. Any small slider bun will work here.

Peel the potatoes and put them into a medium pot of cold water with a pinch of salt. Bring to a boil. When the potatoes are fully cooked, they will be easily pierced with a fork—about 10 to 15 minutes. Drain in a colander and mash using a food mill or a handheld potato ricer or masher.

Chop the cauliflower and carrots into large chunks and place into a food processor. Use the chopping blade to mince the vegetables into an even consistency.

Melt the butter in a large saucepan on medium-high heat. Add the onions and season with a pinch of salt. When the onions begin to soften and appear translucent—about 3 minutes—add the ginger, garlic, and chile. Continue stirring for about 5 more minutes. Then add the masala and cook for another 5 minutes.

Add the minced cauliflower and carrots and continue to stir for about 5 more minutes.

Next, add the tomato paste, peas, and ¼ cup of water. Stir the whole mixture, which will loosen up from the added liquid. Once the tomato paste is fully integrated, add in the mashed potato to thicken.

Fold in the tamarind paste and stir on low heat until all the vegetables are well mixed—about 10 minutes. Season with salt to taste.

To assemble the pavs:
Pile a dollop of the hot veggie mixture on the toasted pavs and top with pickled onions.

VADA PAV, AKA DEEP-FRIED MASHED POTATO SLIDER

Makes about 20 pavs

For the vada:
4 to 6 medium red skin potatoes
2 teaspoons ginger, minced
2 teaspoons serrano chiles, minced
1 teaspoon Toasted Cumin
  (see recipe page 25)
1 teaspoon turmeric powder
½ cup cilantro, roughly chopped
salt to taste

This potato puff pav is also nicknamed the Bombay burger. And it gets well-deserved bragging rights as Mumbai's breakfast of champions. *Vada pav* is a famous dish all over India but especially in Mumbai; it's one of the most popular choices from the street food stalls on Juhu Beach. The traditional *vada*, a well-seasoned potato dumpling, is battered, deep-fried, and sandwiched between pavs slathered with an intense garlic chutney. What's not to like? We use an ice-cream scoop to shape the vada. Our version comes with three chutneys: Tamarind Date Chutney for sweetness, Cilantro Chutney for a bright note, and supercharged Ghost Pepper Chutney for an extra kick.

We use pavs—small slider buns made just for JBC by a local baker. Any small slider bun will work here.

To make the vada:
Peel and quarter the potatoes. Place the potatoes in a stockpot with cold water and a pinch of salt and bring to a boil. When the potatoes are fully cooked—about 10 to 15 minutes—drain in a colander and mash with a food mill or a handheld potato ricer or masher. Let the potato mash cool slightly, about 10 minutes, until it is easy to handle.

Mix in the ginger, chiles, cumin, turmeric, cilantro, and salt. Taste and adjust the salt or spice level, as desired. Portion with a 4-ounce ice-cream scoop; the mix should be slightly bulging over the top of the scoop and not flush with the top. Roll the scoops by hand into smooth balls.

(recipe continues)

For the batter:

2 cups chickpea flour

1 cup warm water

½ teaspoon turmeric powder

½ teaspoon salt

4 to 6 quarts neutral oil
  (for deep-frying)

Ghost Pepper Chutney
  (see recipe page 53)

Tamarind Date Chutney
  (see recipe below, page 53)

Citrus Pickled Onions
  (see recipe page 26)

Cilantro Chutney (see recipe
  page 46)

20 pavs/slider buns

To make the batter:

Whisk together the chickpea flour with the water, turmeric powder, and salt. The batter should be thick, like pancake batter. Heat the oil to 350°F in a heavy-bottom large pot—use a thermometer to make sure the temperature is accurate. Dip the potato balls into the batter one at a time, and then use a spoon to slowly lower the balls into the hot oil. Fry until the batter is crisp and golden—about 5 minutes.

To assemble the pavs:

Spread the ghost pepper chutney on the toasted pavs, and top with a hot fried potato ball. Garnish the ball with tamarind date chutney, followed by pickled onions, and, finally, drizzle with cilantro chutney.

Ghost Pepper Chutney

Makes 1 quart

5 dried ghost peppers
2 cups peeled garlic cloves
2 cups neutral oil
1 cup white wine vinegar
1 cup tomato paste
3 tablespoons salt

We buy our dried ghost peppers from Oaktown Spice Shop on Grand Avenue in Oakland. Find ghost peppers online if there isn't a specialty spice store nearby. This is our spiciest chutney, and it really packs a punch. Ghost peppers are one of the world's spiciest peppers: They are ten times spicier than the habanero. Please wear gloves and use caution when handling these peppers.

Preheat the oven to 350°F. Place the ghost peppers, garlic, and oil in a small oven-safe pan. Cover with aluminum foil and roast for 1 hour. The garlic should be soft and browned on the outside. If the garlic is not totally soft, return to the oven for another 20 minutes. When the roasting is done, let the pan cool for at least 30 minutes.

In a blender, purée the roasted garlic, peppers, oil, and ½ cup water. Pour the mixture into a small stockpot and add the vinegar and tomato paste. Place on medium heat, and stir to fully incorporate the tomato paste for about 15 to 20 minutes. Taste and season with salt. Remove from heat and chill. Store in an airtight container for up to 2 weeks.

Tamarind Date Chutney

Makes 1 cup

1 tablespoon Tamarind Paste
  (see recipe page 23)
3 tablespoons Date Paste
  (see recipe page 25)
1 teaspoon ginger, minced
¼ teaspoon Toasted Cumin
  (see recipe page 25)
¼ teaspoon Indian red chili powder
¼ teaspoon black salt

This ubiquitous sweet and sour condiment can take many forms and interpretations in Indian restaurants and homes. Traditionally the sour tamarind is balanced with the natural sweetness of dates. Many cooks substitute brown sugar or honey to sweeten this dish. But it's the flavor and depth of the dates that really makes this chutney shine.

In a blender, combine the tamarind paste, date paste, ginger, cumin, chili powder, and salt. Add ¼ cup water and blend until smooth. The chutney should be the consistency of ketchup. Add more water if the mixture is too thick.

BOLLYWOOD BALLER PAV,
AKA LAMB MEATBALL SLIDER

Makes 16 to 20 pavs

For the meatballs:

2 slices white bread, crusts cut off

¼ cups whole plain yogurt

2 tablespoons neutral oil

½ large, yellow onion, finely minced

1 tablespoon ginger, minced

1 tablespoons garlic, minced

1 tablespoon serrano chiles, minced

¼ cup Kheema Masala
  (see recipe page 106)

¼ cup tomato paste

2 tablespoons salt

1 pound ground lamb

1 pound ground beef

For the mint chutney:

2 cups fresh mint leaves,
  tightly packed

1 tablespoon garlic, minced

1 cup whole plain yogurt

The meatball sub is king of the carnivore sandwich category, in my humble opinion. This lamb meatball pav is served with a tomato sauce—just like the American version it mimics—but it's seasoned with fresh ginger and curry leaves. Evoking traditionally European flavor pairings, we top the lamb with a mint chutney. The result is a tender meatball sandwich with all the trappings of an Italian meatball slider but a distinctly Indian sensibility.

We use pavs—small slider buns made just for JBC by a local baker. Any small slider bun will work here.

To make the meatballs:

Cut the bread slices into cubes. Whisk the yogurt with ¼ cup water in a small bowl. Add the bread cubes and smash together to soften the bread into a thick porridge-like consistency, and set aside.

Heat the oil in a sauté pan to medium heat, add the onions and a pinch of salt, and stir. After about 3 minutes, when the onions begin to soften and turn translucent, add the ginger, garlic, and chiles. Continue to stir as the aromatics soften—for about 5 minutes. Then add the masala and stir for about 3 minutes. Add in the tomato paste, season with the salt, and cook for an additional 3 minutes, stirring constantly to keep the sauce from sticking. Remove from heat and set aside to cool. When the mixture is cool to the touch—about 20 minutes—fold in the bread mixture.

(recipe continues)

To assemble:

1 quart Curry Leaf Coriander
 Tomato Sauce (see recipe page 235)
20 pavs/slider buns
2 cups Citrus Pickled Onions
 (see recipe page 26)

Preheat the oven to 350°F. In a large bowl mix together the cooled spice mixture and the ground meat. Use your hands to fully combine the ground meat and spices. Roll a small piece into a tiny patty and cook in a sauté pan—for 2 minutes each side. Check the seasoning and add more salt, if needed. Use an ice-cream scoop to portion the meatball mixture equally. Roll into balls by hand. If the meatball mixture is too sticky to handle, rub a small amount of oil on your hands. Place the meatballs on a rack on top of a sheet pan. Put the pan in the oven and cook the meatballs for 15 minutes until they are cooked through. Remove from heat and set aside.

To make the mint chutney:

In a blender combine the mint leaves, garlic, and yogurt. Purée into a thick sauce, and season with salt to taste.

To assemble the pavs:

Heat the curry leaf coriander tomato sauce in a medium saucepan. Add the cooked meatballs and simmer gently for 5 minutes. Toast the pavs on a grill or a broiler until lightly browned. Top each pav with a meatball, pickled onions, and mint chutney.

SHRIMP PO'BHAI

Makes 12 pavs

24 medium shrimp, peeled
  and deveined
1 teaspoon salt
2 tablespoons Chaat Masala
  (see recipe page 106)
½ cup Ginger Curry Leaf Butter
  (see recipe page 177)
20 pavs/slider buns
1 cup Ghost Pepper Yogurt (see recipe
  page 207)
3 cups mixed greens
½ cup Citrus Pickled Onions
  (see recipe page 26)

This pav is a nod to the deliciously sloppy BBQ Shrimp Po'Boy from Liuzza's By The Track in New Orleans. I love NOLA and have visited the city several times. It rates as one of my top food towns anywhere in the world. Liuzza's spin on the classic Louisiana po'boy sandwich is full of buttery peppery shrimp stuffed inside a hollow baguette. The Juhu Beach Club name is a play on the classic: *Bhai* means brother in Gujarati, my parents' first language. We sauté the shrimp in our ginger curry leaf butter and housemade chaat masala.

We use pavs—small slider buns made just for JBC by a local baker. Any small slider bun will work here.

Toss the shrimp with the salt and masala and let the shellfish sit for about 20 minutes. Place a large sauté pan on medium heat, and add the ginger curry leaf butter. When the butter is melted and frothy—but not browning—after about 2 minutes—add the shrimp in an even layer. After about 2 minutes, turn all of the shrimp over and let them cook for 1 more minute. Shake the pan to stop the shrimp from sticking. Cook for 1 more minute and set aside.

To assemble the pavs:
Toast the pavs until lightly browned on a grill or in a broiler. Spread the ghost pepper yogurt on the pavs, place two shrimp on the base of each pav, and drizzle with the seasoned melted butter left in the pan. Top the shrimp with the mixed greens and pickled onions.

PORK BELLY PAV

Makes 12 pavs

For the pork:

3 pounds pork belly, skinless

3 tablespoons Sambar Masala
(see recipe page 109)

2 tablespoons salt

For the tamarind glaze:

2 tablespoons Tamarind Paste
(see recipe page 23)

1 cup granulated sugar

½ cup ginger, minced

Dabeli is a popular vegetarian street food pav in Mumbai. When we first tried this slider, it was a revelation: Spiced mashed potato slathered with chutneys and topped with crunchy garnishes, such as pomegranate seeds, peanuts, and sev. Given the potato base, it reminds me of a "deluxe" Vada Pav. At the restaurant, I wanted to use a different filling than potato, but keep all the toppings that make the dabeli so distinct. Pork belly proved a good fit: The pork is a perfect foil to the sweet and spicy combination of chutneys and crunchy garnishes. Heads-up: This dish requires marinating for several hours.

We use pavs—small slider buns made just for JBC by a local baker. Any small slider bun will work here.

To make the pulled pork:

Place the pork belly on a cutting board, fat side up. Score the fat in long shallow cuts, at a diagonal, about a ¼ inch apart from each other. Make sure not to cut too deeply into the meat. Rub the scored pork belly with the masala and salt to thoroughly coat the meat. Place the pork belly in a shallow, covered container, and refrigerate for at least 12 hours, ideally overnight.

(recipe continues)

To assemble:

2 quarts neutral oil (for deep-frying)

12 pavs/slider buns

½ cup Ghost Pepper Chutney
(see recipe page 53)

½ cup Citrus Pickled Onions
(see recipe page 26)

½ cup Sea Salt Curried Peanuts
(see recipe page 176)

½ cup fresh pomegranate seeds

½ cup Sev (see recipe page 195)

Heat the oven to 350°F. Remove the marinated pork belly from the fridge and place on a sheet pan fitted with a rack. Roast for 1 hour. Increase the temperature to 425°F and continue to roast for another 20 minutes. The skin on the outside of the pork belly should be browned but not burnt. Remove from heat and cool. Once the pork belly is cooled to room temperature—about 30 minutes—wrap it in plastic wrap and chill for at least 4 hours. When the pork belly is fully chilled, remove it from the wrapping and cut into 12 rectangular pieces.

To make the tamarind glaze:

In a medium saucepan, combine the tamarind paste, sugar, ginger, and 2 cups of water. Whisk to incorporate on medium heat, until the sugar and tamarind paste are fully dissolved. When the liquid comes to a boil, lower the heat and let the mix simmer for about 15 minutes to reduce the liquid. The consistency should be like maple syrup but still pourable. Remove from heat and cool to room temperature.

To assemble the pavs:

Heat the oil for deep-frying in a medium saucepan to 375°F. Use a thermometer to check the temperature. Lower a few pieces of the pork belly at a time into the hot oil and fry for about 3 minutes—until the pork belly is crispy on the outside. Remove the pork from the heat and place in a metal bowl. Coat with the tamarind glaze. Toast the pavs until lightly browned on a grill or in a broiler. Brush the pavs with the ghost pepper chutney, top with the glazed pork belly, followed by the onions, peanuts, pomegranate seeds, and sev.

Chapter Two

COMFORT
FOOD

My mom grew up with her nose in a book and didn't learn to cook at home. When she married my dad, she moved to Uganda where his family lived and my grandmother taught her how to cook "the Mistry way." My *ba* (grandmother in Gujarati) was adamant that my mother should know how to cook all the foods my dad was accustomed to eating.

My grandparents moved to Uganda right before my father was born in 1944. The story we were told as kids was that ba was pregnant with my dad on the boat from India. In my head I always imagined this little wooden canoe when in actuality it was a large ship. There was a significant Indian, mainly Gujarati, migration to Uganda throughout the 1940s, '50s, and '60s, when my father was growing up. These immigrants were often shopkeepers and small merchants, like my family, who moved to the large, central Ugandan town of Masaka.

"The Mistry way" of cooking was greatly influenced by the move to this landlocked East African country. Traditional Gujarati food, which is mainly vegetarian, has a reputation for being on the sweet side; you might find a little mashed banana in the pakora

batter, for instance. That's what my mom grew up eating. This could not be further from my father's family's cooking where the focus is on a balance of salt and acid. Also, East African ingredients like cassava and *matoke*, a starchy, green banana that's served cooked, were introduced into the cuisine.

Since my dad grew up in Uganda, there are these dishes he enjoys that are more Indian-African. My dad's family ate *muhogo*—cassava root in Swahili— the way Americans eat potato-based French fries or Latin Americans eat yucca fries. The cassava is steamed, then deep-fried, and in my family it's served with what's known as "public sauce." In this case "the public" refers to the larger family, including kids. Remember, English is a second language for my parents. It's basically a ketchup-based sauce or kitchen sink sauce, doctored with tamarind paste, pickles, minced garlic, lemon juice—whatever is on hand. It's a precursor to my own tamarind ketchup in this book.

My mom eventually mastered these Mistry dishes, and they became an integral part of her repertoire—and our family meals.

When I was growing up, I thought all Gujarati food was like what we ate, until I experienced other Guju families' food and tasted the difference. I like sweet, but I like salt and acid, too.

The Indians in Uganda did quite well for themselves. However, in 1971 there was a military coup, and the brutal dictator Idi Amin seized power as the country's third president. (Uganda gained its independence from Britain in 1962.) Amin fueled an undercurrent of anti-Indian resentment among the indigenous African population. In 1972, he declared that "Africa was for Africans" and ordered all Indians to leave the country in ninety days or face forced expulsion. My family fled, and like the majority of Gujaratis in Uganda who had British passports, they headed to the UK. Something like 60,000 Indians left Uganda then, and almost half relocated to England. It was a massive forced migration.

My family started over in London. That's where I was born. We moved to Wembley, a predominantly Indian enclave in the city's northwest. For almost a decade, my grandparents lived in a household that, for varying amounts of time, also included my parents, my sisters, my aunt and uncle and my cousin, and my two unmarried uncles, who were in their twenties.

Early on, there were eight adults and four kids all in that three-bedroom house. My mother and aunt cooked alongside my grandmother for the whole family. I remember being bathed in the kitchen sink. I had my fifth birthday in that house. My mother, who loved to bake, made a cake in the shape of a five. It was the most impressive thing I'd ever seen.

I didn't know the extent of the family struggle until I was much older. Growing up I just thought grandpa moved to London, became an accountant, went to work for a wealthy man, wore three-piece suits, and smoked Dunhills. He was a pretty cool dude.

But the reality was the family went through very tough times for many years. When they first arrived, my grandparents rented an apartment where the landlord would randomly turn off the heat and tell them they could only shower every other day or he would turn the water off. The cold weather was a shock. My mother got hypothermia in her hands and feet because she didn't understand how cold it was outside and how she needed to bundle up for her health. She'd only known the warmth of India and Uganda. The bone-chilling cold of British winters was foreign to my family.

Not to mention the bone-chilling reception we received in our adopted homeland. I remember skinheads throwing rocks at my family while we tried to have a picnic in the park. It scared and upset me. We had to grab our food and our blanket and make a run for it. The phrase "Pakis go home" was a constant refrain. Racist, ignorant bullies who despise anyone brown or "foreign."

My grandfather initially worked for free to prove to his eventual employer—the wealthy Brit—that he had the qualifications for the job. The man was skeptical at first, but grandpa won him over.

So many Indians have similar stories. It was important to my parents that we understood our history, but they also didn't want to frighten us as children. My dad made us watch the 1981 documentary *Rise and Fall of Idi Amin* every time it came on TV. He could not talk about the pain of hearing his father crying on the phone from Uganda in 1972, but he wanted to make sure we knew what our family had survived.

The Indian diaspora reaches so many places: East Africa, the UK, Trinidad, Fiji, Australia, Hong Kong, and the United States. When people ask me "Where are you from?" I don't know where to start.

The adults in my family tried to protect us as young children from the difficulties of relocating to a strange land. They kept our families' food traditions: Our table was full of samosas, *kachoris*, and other Indian sweet and savory snacks. And there were reasons to celebrate: One of my earliest memories is my uncle's wedding in 1980. The extended family decked out our old cars with colorful garlands for a procession through Wembley to the local hall where he married my aunt. There was a lot of traditional Indian food and dancing and love.

||||||||||||||||||||||||||

Everyone expects me to say that I spent my childhood in the kitchen, tugging on my mom's apron. But that wasn't the case. I'm the youngest of three girls, so I tried to keep *out* of the kitchen as much as possible. As a kid I really just saw cooking as another household chore. I wanted nothing to do with it.

But I *was* really curious about food. My family used to say: "Preeti always wants outside food." That's what they called restaurant food. My parents didn't have much disposable income when I was a kid, so restaurant food was synonymous with extravagance. From my parents' point of view then, I wanted something beyond our means. Honestly, though, I was just curious about the whole restaurant experience: the decor, service, atmosphere, food, drinks—all of it. It was all a mystery, and I wanted in.

When I was young, my sisters and I spent summers in Florida with extended family. My paternal uncle owned electronics stores in Orlando, and I would wake up at six a.m. just to go to work with him every morning. The family said it was only because I wanted

"outside lunch" from places like Subway and Burger King. It was so different from the food we had at home. To begin with, the places I was drawn to were shrines to meat. Even if they'd had the money, my vegetarian parents wouldn't have paid to eat at burger joints or restaurants like Ponderosa Steak House and Red Lobster.

Now I love all the vegetarian Indian food that my mom makes. And I make a lot of it, too, at the restaurant. But growing up I was like—argh! that's all we ever eat: the same Gujarati food every week.

I wanted to try other flavors and other foods. In the shopping center that housed one of my uncle's stores there was also a particular restaurant that piqued my interest. I can still remember it; I must have been about nine at the time. I don't think I'd ever been to an independent restaurant quite like it. It was fancy: there was a fountain in the front foyer and a menu on the window.

They didn't serve lunch, but I could look inside. The very fact that it wasn't open for lunch made it special! They made crab cakes and oysters. I had no idea what those were or what they tasted like. It was so intriguing to me. I never did eat there. I think I thought it of it as a place that served "real" American cuisine. Not that I really had any concept of cuisine, whether French, Chinese, Vietnamese, Thai, or even American for that matter.

On the rare occasion we went out to eat (mainly to Mexican or Italian restaurants for the most vegetarian options), I always wanted the most expensive thing on the menu, like the chicken fajita platter, a giant plate that I could never finish. My parents weren't hard-liners: I was allowed to order meat off the menu if I wanted to, and I was all about burgers and bacon back then. Luckily, my dad or one of my older sisters would come to my rescue if I over-ordered. Waste was frowned upon in our house. I really just wanted a few bites of meat to match my tiny kid appetite.

I wanted it because it was different. And I was hungry for more.

|||||||||||||||||||||||||

I was my mom's little baby, the youngest. You might even say I was the favorite—certainly until puberty. I spent a lot of time hanging out with her when my older sisters went to school. In our kitchen we had a dining table and a little TV. When I was older, after school I'd be sitting there doing homework, playing video games, or watching TV while she cooked. We were in the same space, but we were doing our own things. She was always multitasking: the pressure cooker would be on, she'd have beans or lentils soaking, and she'd be grinding spices for the next day.

I was like the boy my mom didn't have: I'd do all those so-called masculine-type jobs for her, like take out the trash and clean up the big mess in the kitchen when the lid of the pressure cooker flew off and dal hit the ceiling—that's a true story. I'd go grocery shopping with mom at the Indian store in Toledo. She knew where to go to get bitter gourds, chiles, curry leaves, Indian eggplants, lentils, chickpea flour, and, of course, whole spices.

The food wasn't exciting to me because it's what I knew. I didn't see the novelty in it or what I value in it now because I don't eat that way every single day of the week. There's a spiced yogurt soup called *kadhi* that I hated as a kid; now I admire the technique that goes into making it and the supersour flavor. Most of the soups my mom made were lentil-based, generally with tomato, onion, and garlic in the mix. But kadhi has a base that is essentially a roux made with chickpea flour and yogurt that is thickened with hot oil and aromatics.

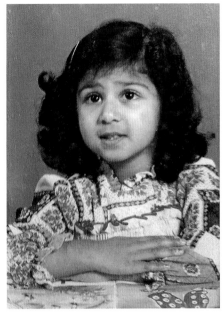

As a kid it seemed weird compared to the soups we had most nights. The sour yogurt taste made me pucker up uncomfortably. It wasn't the only dish I didn't care for. There was an okra and potato shaak that my mom made on a regular basis. I would try to move the okra to the side and only eat the potatoes; my pint-sized palate couldn't get past the slime factor with okra. When you're a kid, there are just some tastes and textures that are a harder sell. And my mom didn't ever tone down the spice. I used to eat my dinner with a pint glass of milk every night. We learned to appreciate heat in my childhood home.

These days, it's different when I go back to Ohio. Sometimes I cook for my mom. She loves that. I made a surprise visit for her seventieth birthday in 2016 and cooked for my parents and a bunch of their friends. I made my versions of some of my mom's favorite dishes: *sev puri*, vegetarian *biryani*, and pav bhaji. I grew up eating the food prepared by the Indian women who attended that birthday dinner; now they ask me for recipes. To this day, though, my mom has no problem telling me if I'm using too much flour to roll out the puris or when I'm not cooking the rice "the right way." It's a healthy exchange around culinary techniques . . . most of the time.

And I still love it when she cooks for me. There's a vegetable shaak called *giloda* made with ivy gourds: small, scarlet gourds that taste like bitter melon. There's an acrid sharpness on the tongue from the ivy gourds that's unlike other fruits or vegetables. My mom makes a dry sauté with the ivy gourds, potatoes, and spices such as turmeric and her secret ingredient: a little ketchup. It was a Monday night dish. Now, when I go home, it doesn't matter what day of the week it is, she'll make it for me. I can seriously throw down a big bowl of giloda along with a half dozen of her rotli (also known as roti), thin, light, fluffy unleavened bread. That meal transports me right back to the family table. It's like I'm twelve years old again. I know how happy it makes my mom to see that no matter that I'm now a professional chef, I still love her cooking.

Sunday nights were special. Mom made a delicious dish called *ravaiya*, with little baby eggplants and potatoes roasted in a spice blend of cumin, coriander, and raw peanuts; there are all these different tastes and textures going on. I'm always drawn to lots of layering of flavors in a dish. Mom split the eggplants, stuffed them with the masala, and roasted them in the oven; the smell used to waft through the whole house. Then she'd finish the dish by adding a little water to pick up all the spices that had caramelized on the bottom of the pan (what's known as deglazing the pan

in French cuisine) to make a thick sauce that coated the vegetables.

My sisters and I swore it tasted like chicken. Instead of calling it ravaiya we called it chicken-stuffed potatoes. It's like the ultimate homey, comfort food served up on a Sunday night. We'd have it with *masala chass*, a savory lassi that's popular at street food stands and in five-star restaurants. It's made with yogurt and salt and comes with a tempering on top; you sizzle oil with garlic, cumin seeds, or curry leaves, drizzle it really fast on the drink, and then mix it in. It's a favorite cooling drink that pairs well with hot dishes. And we'd have *kitcheri*, a thick porridge of gently spiced rice and split mung beans. It's belly-warming food that sustains you for the week ahead.

Sundays were also the day mom made her signature snacks. Things like *patra*—a classic Gujarati snack—lots of non-Gujarati Indians don't even know these spicy, steamed taro leaf treats. They're so good: with their medley of complementary flavors in the filling, such as tangy spicy chile and sharp ginger. You start with huge taro leaves and split the vein out. And then you make a paste with chickpea flour, water, oil, spices, and ground peanuts. You spread the paste on the leaf and roll the whole thing up: it looks like an oversize dolma. Then you steam the rolls.

After they're cooked, you can slice them and eat as is. But my mom would go the extra mile: she'd quickly sauté the slices in garlic, mustard seeds, and curry leaves. It's crispier and more flavorful than the simply steamed version. I can happily chow down on these little pinwheels any day of the week. When my family lived in Pittsburgh when I was five, there was a guy who delivered taro leaves to our door. These are specialty ingredients even within our community. It's easier for someone to have a side project and bring them to you than to have to track them down all over the place.

You can buy Indian patra canned, just like Greek dolmas. Even some Gujarati people I know have only had the canned version. They're nowhere near as good. They lack the pliable texture of fresh patra and have less flavor.

I never saw a can in our pantry growing up. I didn't know that was unusual. It's all I knew. I guess in that way you could say my mom's influence is all over the Juhu Beach Club menu.

As a child, my friends were amazed by the rows of glass jars in my mom's pantry filled with spices and lentils. Not me: I was bored by it as a kid. I wanted

novelty: after school I'd heat up a frozen Stouffer's French Bread Pizza or a can of Campbell's Chicken Noodle Soup that I picked up myself, doctoring it up with whatever I could find in my mom's pantry like garlic powder, lemon pepper, or minced ginger. That felt both familiar and exciting, exotic.

Now when I go home, I gorge on what my mom makes; I can't believe how much delicious food she made us, every night, when I was a kid.

Some of the items on my restaurant's menu are inspired by my mom's dishes. And many of them are some of my wife Ann's favorite foods now, too.

The fried rice at Juhu Beach Club is like my mom's. Only hers has no bacon in it. And we put in a lot of seasonal vegetables. I also add mango for some salty-sweetness. But the basics—curry leaves, mustard seeds, turmeric, traditional veggies (potatoes, peas, cauliflower)—are the same.

I touch base with my mom about certain dishes or spice blends, but then I make them my own. The Guju Chili in this chapter is pretty similar to her's, but she doesn't purée the dish, as I do. Mom's version is much chunkier than mine. She's eaten at the restaurant. I think she thinks I've done alright.

KITCHEN
BEGINNINGS

I didn't start cooking until I left home.

I met Ann in a bar in Ann Arbor in February 1996. I moved there at eighteen because I had dropped out of Bowling Green State University and my sister was in school at the University of Michigan at Ann Arbor. I was supposed to go to community college, but I flaked. I got barista jobs instead. I was all about my black leather jacket, eight-hole combat boots, and shaved head. The first time my mother saw my bald head, she said I'd "murdered the happiness." As I mentioned, English is her second language, but still.

Ann had this cute little pixie cut. She wore combat boots, too. I was nineteen, she was twenty-two. We fell in love. Six months later we decided to move to San Francisco together. That was back in 1996. I went to New College and studied film. Ann went to San Francisco State University to get her MBA.

We were broke. We basically survived on burritos and pizza by the slice. That got old pretty quickly. I realized I had to cook at home, and so I just started making stuff.

Back then, Ann and I were both vegetarian. It was the '90s. So I made a lot of things like pasta fagioli because I thought it was the grown-up version of minestrone. My go-to cookbooks during that period: *Williams-Sonoma Vegetarian*, *Martha Stewart Hors d'Oeuvres Handbook*, anything by Deborah Madison.

I shopped at Bi-Rite, a corner market reinvented as a gourmet grocery store in the Mission District neighborhood where we lived. That place was a culinary education. I'd survey everything first, pick whatever vegetables looked best, and then go home and experiment. I'd make baked polenta with mushroom ragout or asparagus risotto, probably still with store-bought vegetable stock. I was just getting started.

We couldn't afford to go to fancy restaurants, so we had celebrations at home with friends. We got to be well known among our circle for throwing great parties. We both like to host.

Ann has a cool aesthetic: she'd put flowers on the table, make place cards for everyone, and get quirky napkin holders from a thrift store. We paired wines with the food. We were enamored with the whole thing. We were young. It was our first taste of freedom. We'd dress up: I wore vintage store suits and ties. Ann wore cute pencil skirts. It was fun playing grown-ups.

One of the most memorable nights was a ten-course dinner we did in 1999 to ring in the millennium. The main course had roasted eggplant rounds with edible flowers. My sister Meenal was drying lettuce out on the dining table because my kitchen was too small for such maneuvers. We began the evening with a cheese fondue and ended it with a chocolate one. Ann had started collecting vintage fondue pots; since

then she's expanded her collecting to include all sorts of vintage dishes, cups, and cookware. Many of these dishes eventually find their way to JBC.

Then, later that spring, I got invited to a Passover seder, and I had to bring something to share. People had come to expect I would make something substantial, a main dish. I felt the responsibility of that.

I made a vegetable biryani, my mom's recipe with a twist: I mixed a third of the rice with grated carrot and a third with spinach so it made an Indian flag. I used cloves to make the little *chakra* or spoke wheel in the middle.

Even though I was still discon-nected from my culture, I was proud of it, too. I was going to something new

to me—a Jewish holiday feast—and I wanted to share something of myself with my new friends; nobody else in the crowd was of Indian heritage.

I woke up at six a.m. to make it before class and carefully put the Pyrex glass dish in the fridge before I left for school. I was so pleased with the end result and the reaction it got. I'm a Libra, a people pleaser. It felt good doing something people enjoyed.

And it was a first step toward what would eventually evolve into my cooking philosophy at the restaurant: inventive, rustic, family style, aesthet-ically pleasing, a nod to my past, and an acknowledgment of my present.

I didn't know it back then, but that was the beginning of something.

FRUIT CHAAT

Serves 4

½ bulb fresh fennel

1 cup Greek yogurt (we use Straus)

1 teaspoon Toasted Cumin
   (see recipe page 25)

1 teaspoon Indian red chili powder

½ teaspoon salt

¼ cup pistachios, shelled

variety of seasonal fruits, sliced
   or halved (We use at least 3 kinds
   of fruit, for example: melon,
   nectarine, and strawberry in
   the summer; or apples, persimmons,
   and kiwis in the fall.)

¼ cup Tamarind Citrus Vinaigrette
   (see recipe page 173)

¼ cup Tamarind Date Chutney
   (see recipe page 53)

¼ cup Cilantro Chutney
   (see recipe page 46)

1 ripe avocado

All over the streets of Mumbai stalls sell fruit with chile or chaat masala. Those stands are the reference point for this fruit chaat. The recipe calls for two chutneys and a vinaigrette we make from scratch. I recommend making this recipe in conjunction with another dish—such as a pav or the Bhel Salad—that uses these chutneys. The key here is to use the best seasonal fruit; that's what makes this dish a standout.

Thinly slice the fennel bulb lengthwise with a mandoline or sharp knife. Place the fennel slices in a small bowl with cold water to cover. Set aside. Mix the yogurt with the cumin, chili powder, and salt. Set aside.

Preheat the oven to 350°F. Place the pistachios on a small sheet pan and toast them in the oven until they are slightly browned and crunchy. When the pistachios have cooled, roughly chop them, and set aside.

Toss the fruits and fennel with the tamarind vinaigrette. Spread the yogurt mixture on the bottom of a plate. Drizzle the yogurt with the tamarind and cilantro chutneys. Arrange the dressed fennel and fruit on top of the yogurt and chutneys to create a small pile on each plate. Slice the avocado and arrange equally on each plate. Sprinkle with the pistachios. Serve immediately.

HEIRLOOM TOMATO SALAD

Serves 4

1 cup Greek yogurt (we use Straus)

1 teaspoon turmeric powder

1 teaspoon Toasted Cumin
   (see recipe page 25)

½ tablespoon salt

4 to 6 medium heirloom tomatoes,
   cut into large wedges

½ pint cherry tomatoes, halved

**For the green goddess
   dressing:**

2 cloves garlic

1 bunch chives, roughly chopped
   (reserve two for garnish)

1 bunch tarragon, leaves
   picked and roughly chopped

2 tablespoons whole plain yogurt

¼ cup white wine vinegar

1 teaspoon salt

1 teaspoon freshly ground
   black pepper

1 cup neutral oil

In my mind, the arrival of heirloom tomatoes at the farmers' market signals the official start to summer. In this recipe, the tomato itself is the star—with a little assistance from the Indian spice pantry. I like to mix a few different varieties of cherry tomatoes in with the large heirloom tomatoes—of various sizes and colors—to really emphasize the diversity of choices during peak tomato season. We top it with our take on green goddess dressing.

Mix the yogurt, turmeric, and cumin in a small bowl. Season with ½ tablespoon of salt and set aside.

To make the dressing:
Place the garlic, chives, tarragon, yogurt, and vinegar in a blender and purée until smooth. Add the salt and pepper. Pour the oil into a running blender in a slow steady stream. The dressing will emulsify into a creamy light green vinaigrette.

To assemble the salad:
Spread the turmeric yogurt on the bottom of each plate. Toss the tomatoes with the vinaigrette and a pinch of salt. Then arrange the tomatoes on top of the yogurt. Finely chop the two remaining chives and sprinkle them on top of the dressed tomatoes. Serve immediately.

MOM'S GUJU CHILI

Makes 2 quarts

1 cup moong (mung) beans
¼ cup neutral oil
½ tablespoon cumin seeds
½ yellow onion, julienned
1 tablespoon garlic, minced
1 tablespoon, ginger minced
1 tablespoon serrano chile, minced
1 tablespoon Dhanna Jeeru Masala
   (see recipe page 102)
1 cup tomato paste
2 cups puréed whole tomatoes,
   or roughly chopped fresh tomato
1 lemon, juiced
2 tablespoons salt

My family has a tradition of cooking the same meal on a particular day of the week. Not just my parents, but my whole extended Mistry family eats pretty much a similar menu on Sundays, Mondays, Tuesdays, and so on. In my home growing up, Wednesday was always *moong dal*, a hearty lentil soup. My mom would soak the *moong* (mung) beans Tuesday night. I eat this dish for lunch at least twice a week. Many people are shocked to find out the soup contains no meat, since it has such a meaty texture—like chili. Hence its name here.

Soak the dried moong beans in room temperature water for at least 12 hours, ideally overnight.

Heat the oil in a medium stockpot on medium-high heat. Add the cumin seeds and onions and stir as the onions begin to soften. After the onions start to slightly brown—in about 5 to 7 minutes—add the garlic, ginger, and chiles and stir to mix.

After another 5 minutes—when the garlic, ginger, and chiles begin to brown and slightly stick to the bottom of the pan—add the masala. Stir the tomato paste with 2 cups of water, and use the liquid to help release any spices stuck to the bottom of the pot. Mix thoroughly to blend in the tomato paste.

Add the tomato purée, moong beans, and enough water to ensure all ingredients are covered. Mix thoroughly, and increase heat to bring the soup to a boil. When the soup boils, reduce the temperature to medium low and let it simmer until the moong beans are fully cooked, about 20 to 30 minutes.

Remove the soup from the heat and purée it with a handheld immersion blender. Or let the soup cool slightly and then purée it in batches in a blender. Then return the soup to the stockpot, add the lemon juice, and heat before serving. Taste and add salt as needed. Store the cooled leftovers in an airtight container in the refrigerator for up to a week.

TOMATO SHORBA

Makes 2 quarts

2 tablespoons Ghee (see recipe
   page 22)
2 cloves
½ tablespoon cumin seeds
¼ cup fresh curry leaves
6 cups (1½ quarts) canned
   tomato purée
½ tablespoon black pepper,
   freshly ground
1 tablespoon ginger, minced
1 teaspoon Indian red chili powder
1 tablespoon salt

My mother made this soup for me whenever I got sick.
It's tangy, spicy, and clears the sinuses. This is pure
comfort food. It's one of less than a handful of JBC
recipes I have not adapted in some way. This *shorba*
is exactly like the soup my mother made for me when I
was a sniffling ten-year-old.

Heat the ghee on high in a medium stockpot. Add the whole
spices and let them sizzle for about 1 minute.

Add the curry leaves and stir to fry the leaves for another
minute; take care not to burn them. When the leaves are crispy
but not blackened, add the tomato purée and 1 cup of water.

Stir in the black pepper, ginger, and chili powder. Taste the
soup and season with salt as needed. Simmer for about 10
minutes before serving. Store the cooled leftovers in an airtight
container in the refrigerator for up to a week.

COCONUT CARROT GINGER SOUP

Makes 4 quarts

2 tablespoons neutral oil

1 large yellow onion, julienned

3 tablespoons ginger, minced

1 tablespoon serrano chile, minced

2 tablespoons Dhanna Jeeru
  Masala (see recipe page 102)

12 large carrots

1 teaspoon turmeric powder

2 cans coconut milk
  (we use Chaokoh brand)

1 tablespoon Tamarind Paste
  (see recipe page 23)

This soup dates back to one of my first jobs in the culinary industry at London's Sugar Club restaurant, working under Australian chef David Selex. David's fall squash soup included lemongrass and coconut. I could not get enough of this as a young cook. The magical combination of coconut milk and a souring agent stuck in my head. In this recipe, we swap out the lemongrass for tamarind. The result is a tangy soup with a distinctly Indian thread, thanks to the spices.

Heat the oil in a medium stockpot on medium-high heat. Add the onion and season it with a pinch of salt. Once the onion begins to soften—in about 3 to 5 minutes—add the ginger, chiles, and masala mixture. Stir for another 5 minutes.

Peel the carrots and chop them into 1-inch pieces. Add the carrots, turmeric, and coconut milk to the pot. Use the liquid from the coconut milk to scrape the spices from the bottom of the pot. Add a canful of water to cover the vegetables and the tamarind paste. Bring the liquid to a boil, then reduce to low heat. Cover and simmer for about 20 minutes or until the carrots are soft.

Let the mixture cool. Blend the soup in batches in a traditional blender or with an immersion blender. When the soup is puréed, run it through a sieve to ensure the texture is smooth. The soup should be thick and creamy. Season it with salt to taste. Store the cooled leftovers in an airtight container in the refrigerator for up to a week.

BOMBAY SANDWICH

Makes 6 sandwiches

1 medium gold beet

1 tablespoon neutral oil

1 medium Yukon Gold potato

1 loaf of white Pullman bread or Pan di Mie

Cilantro Chutney (see recipe page 46)

Citrus Pickled Onions (see recipe page 26)

3 cups grated Monterey Jack cheese

Chaat Masala (see recipe page 106)

½ cup Ghee (see recipe page 22)

A sought-after street food sandwich, this dish is also served in many Bombay (Mumbai) cafes. It is an adult-friendly, Indian-spiced grilled cheese that is in many ways more than the sum of its parts: cheese, beets, chutney, potato, pickled onions, and chaat masala. It takes many of our Indian customers back to the streets of Mumbai in a few bites. At JBC we serve this sandwich with our Tomato Shorba—like the classic American combo of grilled cheese and tomato soup. Only our version has a few more bells and whistles and a bigger flavor kick. A panini press is helpful here; or use a saucepan lid to press the sandwich on the stove.

Preheat the oven to 350°F. Scrub the beet to remove any excess dirt. Place the beet in a small oven-safe pan and drizzle it with oil. Season the beet lightly with salt and fill the pan about a ½ inch from the bottom with water. Cover tightly with aluminum foil and roast it in the oven for about 40 minutes, or until the beet is fully cooked and easily pierced with a small paring knife. When the beet has cooled, peel and thinly slice into rounds. Set aside.

Scrub the potato, place in a small saucepan, and fill the saucepan with cold water to cover. Place the pan on high heat and bring the water to a boil. After the water boils, lower the temperature to medium and continue to simmer until the potato is just cooked through—about 7 to 10 minutes. Remove the pan from the heat and remove the potato from the water with a spoon or tongs. Let the potato cool fully on a sheet pan at room temperature. Then peel the potato and thinly slice it into rounds. Set aside.

(recipe continues)

To assemble the sandwich:

Slice the bread into 12 equally thick slices. (Save the bread ends for breadcrumbs). Drizzle each slice with a tablespoon of cilantro chutney. Build the vegetables on half the slices starting with a layer of beets, followed by potatoes, and then top with a tablespoon of pickled onions spread across the potato. Sprinkle a ½ cup of cheese on the other half of the bread slices.

Heat the oven broiler to high. Place the bread slices open faced on a sheet pan. Sprinkle each slice with about 1 tablespoon chaat masala and a pinch of salt. Place the pan under the broiler until the cheese is fully melted—about 3 minutes. Remove from the broiler and place each melted cheese bread slice on top of a vegetable bread slice.

Heat a nonstick sauté pan or griddle to medium. Brush both sides of the sandwiches with ghee and place them on the pan or griddle. Use a steak press or saucepan lid to press down on each sandwich. When the bottom of a sandwich is well browned and toasted, flip and repeat until both sides are browned. Alternatively, simply place each sandwich in a panini press. Remove from heat, cut into triangles, and serve warm.

ZUCCHINI FRITTERS

Makes 24 fritters

2 pounds zucchini

2 pounds Yukon Gold potatoes

1 serrano chile, minced

2 inches of ginger, peeled and minced

2 tablespoons Toasted Cumin
   (see recipe page 25)

2 cups semolina

1 tablespoon salt

2 tablespoons neutral oil

Coconut Chutney (see recipe
   page 127)

Cherry Tomato Chutney
   (recipe follows, page 86)

These fritters—crisp on the outside and soft on the inside—make a perfect summertime snack, when zucchini is in abundant supply. Also plentiful in this season: the cherry tomatoes used in the accompanying chutney recipe. The coconut chutney adds some heat to the whole experience. These fritters have a lot going on: A crispy, spicy, tangy, sweet, savory, and salty flavor bomb in one bite.

Use a box grater to grate the zucchini on the largest grate size. Season the grated zucchini with 2 pinches of salt and place it in a large sieve or over a large bowl to drain the excess liquid. Let the zucchini sit for at least 10 minutes. Then squeeze the zucchini by hand and press down on the sieve to remove any excess liquid.

Peel the potatoes and place them in a saucepan filled with cold water and a pinch of salt. Heat the saucepan to high, and bring the water to a boil. Cook the potatoes until they are easily pierced by a small paring knife—about 10 minutes. Drain the potatoes and push them through a potato ricer or mash them with a potato masher until creamy.

In a large bowl combine the grated zucchini and the mashed potato. Fold in the chile, ginger, cumin, and a few pinches of salt to taste. Dust a sheet pan with the semolina and reserve the excess semolina in another pan for dredging or coating. Use an ice-cream scoop to make 4-ounce balls of fritter mix. Place on the semolina-dusted pan. Once all of the mixture is scooped, dredge each ball through the excess semolina to fully coat the fritters. Pat down the coated patties and set aside.

In a nonstick or cast-iron skillet, heat the oil on medium high. Cook the fritters in the pan in batches until all are browned and crispy—about 3 minutes each side.

To assemble:
Spread the coconut chutney on the bottom of a plate or platter, stack the fritters next, and top with the cherry tomato chutney.

Cherry Tomato Chutney

Makes 1 quart

2 tablespoons neutral oil
½ tablespoon cumin seeds
½ tablespoon nigella seeds
   (also known as onion seeds)
¼ cup fresh curry leaves
¼ cup ginger, minced
½ tablespoon Indian red
   chili powder
1 teaspoon turmeric powder
2 pints cherry tomatoes, halved
¼ cup granulated sugar
¼ cup white wine vinegar
1 tablespoon salt

This chutney is a marriage of a California-style compote I have had in my repertoire for several years and a traditional Indian tomato *kalonji* (onion seed) chutney. After experimenting with a number of tomato chutney recipes that were mainly a thick purée similar to ketchup, I decided to combine the chunky texture of my compote with the aromatics that make this tomato chutney fiery and unique. This chutney is an ideal condiment served alongside cheese and crackers, grilled meat, or fish.

Heat the oil in a sauté pan on medium high with the cumin, nigella seeds, and curry leaves. When the seeds begin to slightly brown, add the ginger and stir frequently, for about a minute or so. Add the chili powder, turmeric, and tomatoes. Scrape the bottom of the pan with the juices from the tomatoes. Add the sugar, vinegar, and salt. Simmer for about 10 minutes on medium heat to reduce the liquid. Let cool, and store in an airtight container in the refrigerator for up to a week.

CHUMPCHI'S CHANNA
WITH EGGS & SAUSAGE

Makes 4 servings

For the channa:

1 cup black chickpeas

2 tablespoons neutral oil

½ yellow onion, julienned

1 teaspoon garlic, minced

1 teaspoon ginger, minced

1 teaspoon serrano chiles, minced

¼ cup JBC Garam Masala
  (see recipe page 103)

½ cup tomato paste

1 tablespoon salt

For the sausage:

½ pound ground pork

2 teaspoons salt

1 teaspoon ginger, minced

1 teaspoon garlic, minced

1 teaspoon Toasted Cumin
  (see recipe page 25)

¼ cup packed roughly chopped
  cilantro

1 tablespoon neutral oil

This dish is named after my wife Ann, whose nickname is Chumpchi. In Gujarati *chumpchi* literally means "spoon," but the slang definition describes a person who is a little cheeky, almost even pushy—but still operates within the bounds of good intention. The dish itself embodies a lot of what my lovely wife seeks in a hearty brunch: warm, spicy, black chickpeas, pork sausage, and runny yolks. Like a chumpchi this dish is almost over the top but errs on the side of soul-satisfying goodness.

To make the channa:

Soak the chickpeas in a bowl in cold water at room temperature for at least 6 hours, ideally overnight. Heat the oil in a large saucepan on medium high until it is hot—about 1 minute. Add the onion and season it with salt. After about 3 minutes, when the onion begins to soften, add the garlic, ginger, and chiles. Stir to combine for about 2 minutes, then add the masala and tomato paste. Continue to stir for about 5 minutes, and then add 4 cups of water. Stir to fully incorporate and scrape bits from the bottom of the pan. Strain the water from the chickpeas and add them to the pot. Simmer for about 30 minutes, until the chickpeas are fully cooked.

(recipe continues)

For the garnish:
1 cup Greek yogurt
¼ teaspoon Toasted Cumin
  (see recipe page 25)
¼ teaspoon Indian red chili powder

To assemble:
8 cage-free eggs
Citrus Pickled Onions
  (see recipe page 26)
Sev (see recipe page 195)

To make the sausage:

Preheat the oven to 350°F. Combine all the ingredients in a bowl and mix to fully incorporate. Break off a small piece of the sausage and fry it in a sauté pan. Check for seasoning, and add more salt if needed. Separate the sausage mix into 12 evenly sized pieces and form them into small patties. Place the sausage patties on a rack fitted over a sheet pan and cook the patties in the oven for about 10 to 15 minutes, until the meat is cooked all the way through.

To season the yogurt:

Mix the yogurt with the toasted cumin and chili powder and set aside.

To assemble the dish:

Heat a nonstick skillet on medium and fry the eggs, two at a time, sunny-side up. Spoon the warm channa into 4 shallow bowls. Top with 2 fried eggs, and nestle 3 hot sausage patties next to the eggs. Garnish with the seasoned yogurt, pickled onions, and sev.

JBC CLASSIC CHICKEN CURRY

Serves 4

4 whole chicken legs or
  1 whole chicken

For the marinade:
2 cloves garlic, minced
2 tablespoons ginger, minced
2 inches of fresh turmeric root,
  minced (or substitute 1 teaspoon
  powdered turmeric)
2 serrano chiles, minced
1 bunch cilantro (including stems),
  roughly chopped
1 tablespoon Mustard Fenugreek
  Masala (see recipe page 102)
1 tablespoon salt

For the sauce:
3 tablespoons neutral oil
½ yellow onion, julienned
1 tablespoon ginger, minced
½ tablespoon serrano chile, minced
2 cups green cabbage, julienned
1 tablespoon Dhanna Jeeru Masala
  (see recipe page 102)
2 cups canned diced tomatoes

Chicken curry Sunday has been a thing my wife Ann and I have been hosting for several years now. It started as a way to have friends over to share a simple homey dinner. We make the marinade the night before, and once all the ingredients are in the pot the next day, we just let the chicken simmer, filling the house with an appealing aroma. I prefer to use chicken legs because they braise well, remaining tender on the bone. If you are using a whole chicken, add the breast meat half-way through the braising process to avoid making the meat tough and chewy. If desired, I recommend adding hearty vegetables like potatoes, carrots, kale, or chard for a one-pot dinner.

To marinate the chicken:
Remove the skin from the chicken legs. Place the garlic, ginger, turmeric, chile, cilantro, masala, and salt in a blender with ½ cup of water. Purée the mixture until fully incorporated; it should be the consistency of pesto. Pour the marinade over the chicken legs, mix to ensure the chicken is fully coated, and let it sit for at least 6 hours, or ideally overnight.

To braise the chicken:
Heat the oil in a large saucepan. Add the onion and a pinch of salt and let simmer on medium-high heat to soften the onions. When the onions begin to release liquid—in about 5 to 7 minutes—add the ginger and chile. After a few minutes, add the cabbage and masala and stir. A little bit of the spice blend will stick to the bottom of the pan; this is normal. Continue to stir and after about 3 minutes add the tomatoes and 1 cup of water. Scrape the bottom of the pan with a spoon to remove any spices and mix them into the sauce.

Season the sauce with salt to taste, and stir to fully combine all the ingredients. Add the chicken and all of the marinade. Make sure the chicken is fully covered in the sauce, add a little extra water if needed, and bring to a boil. After the sauce comes to a boil, lower the heat and cover for 20 to 25 minutes. To check the chicken's readiness, pull out a leg with a pair of tongs. If it is fully cooked, the meat should pull away from the bone. If not, let it simmer for a few more minutes until the chicken is fully cooked. Remove the chicken from the heat and set aside.

The sauce should be thick and chunky. If it is too soupy, place the pan on medium heat to reduce the liquid and ensure a thicker sauce consistency. Return the chicken to the hot sauce to warm. Serve over lemon turmeric rice.

ASPARAGUS NEST

Makes 4 servings

For the fenugreek salsa verde:
2 stalks green garlic
1 cup fresh fenugreek leaves
1 cup white wine vinegar
½ cup neutral oil
1 tablespoon pepper, freshly ground
1 teaspoon salt

For the nest:
4 duck eggs
1 bunch asparagus, tough
    stems removed
2 tablespoons unsalted butter
1 teaspoon ginger, finely minced
1 tablespoon Preserved Meyer Lemons
    (see recipe page 27)
2 tablespoons Chaat Masala
    (see recipe page 106)
2 sprigs mint, finely chopped

Asparagus season marks the beginning of spring, and nothing says spring like this dish. This is so JBC: seasonal, Indian-influenced, inventive, yet rooted in tradition. I have always loved the classic European pairing of asparagus and egg. One ingredient note: Look for fresh fenugreek leaves at local Indian or Asian markets. Substitute either dried or frozen fenugreek in a pinch. But—heads-up—there is really no substitute for the fresh leaves and their unique, grassy flavor.

Remove the outer leaves of the green garlic and finely mince the white part of the bulb. Pick the fenugreek leaves off the stem and finely mince the leaves. Whisk the garlic and fenugreek with the vinegar, oil, pepper, and salt to taste.

Bring a large saucepan of water to boil. After the water boils, lower the duck eggs into it for 6 minutes. Fill a bowl big enough for the eggs with ice water. Once cooked, remove the eggs from the saucepan and plunge them into ice-cold water immediately. When cooled—about 5 minutes—peel the eggs and set them aside.

Chop the asparagus into 2-inch pieces. In a sauté pan heat the butter until it starts to brown, add the ginger, and let it soften for about 1 minute. Add the asparagus and sauté until the asparagus is cooked through but still firm—about 5 to 7 minutes, depending on their thickness. Dice preserved Meyer lemon and add to the asparagus. Season the asparagus with chaat masala and salt to taste.

To assemble:
Place the asparagus in a circle on plates, to create a "nest." Put a soft-cooked duck egg in the center. Drizzle the nest with the fenugreek salsa verde and garnish with mint.

Chapter Three

MASALA
MASHUPS

My nose lets me know when I'm getting close to the restaurant: Especially when I ride my bike to work, fragrant spices start to waft my way a few blocks before I reach Juhu Beach Club. This welcoming aroma fills the neighborhood. It gets me stoked before I even walk in the door.

I haven't always been a DIY spice maker. I had to find my own way, in my own time, to the superiority of roasting and grinding my own spices for house-made masalas.

When I first started cooking Indian food in my early twenties at home in San Francisco, I just bought boxed mas-alas from the local Indian grocery store. I'd add these premade spice blends to whatever vegetables and protein I had on hand. Those little packets that line an entire aisle offered so many choices: Channa Masala, Pav Bhaji Masala, Chicken Masala, Lamb Kheema Masala—the promise of a delicious dinner stored inside a container. They were like magic boxes that could trans-form any dish from ho-hum to instant hit. It was quick and convenient. I never really stopped to think about doing it any other way.

My aha moment—call it my masala epiphany—came when I didn't have the spice package in the pantry to make pav bhaji at home. Ann and I were both hungry, we had the vegetables to make the dish, but not the little box of masala. So I grabbed a cookbook off the shelf and looked up a recipe.

That's when I realized I already had all the spices to make the masala from scratch. Digging through my pantry shelf I found jars of coriander, cumin, cardamom, cloves, fenugreek seeds, mustard seeds, black salt, dried mango powder, black peppercorns. So first I measured out these whole spices, in the amounts the recipe advised, and then I ground them in a coffee grinder I used for grinding pepper, cumin, and a few other spices. It took all of fifteen minutes.

Then I went about my usual busi-ness making the bhaji and assembling the pavs. When Ann and I sat down to dinner, we took two bites and then looked at each other like we'd made a profound discovery. It was like eating a real tomato—the in-season, organic, freshly picked kind—for the first time. In other words, a revelation. As we ate, we talked about the different spice notes and nuances we could smell and taste in each bite and how much more com-plex the flavors were compared to the

box-made version. There was no comparison. Duh, right?

That was a turning point in my culinary exploration. Once you've tasted that kind of difference in your own cooking, there's no turning back.

I never used one of those premade blends again.

⸻

Spices are the soul of Juhu Beach Club cooking. Our clipboard listing all the masala recipes on our menu? That's the keys to the kingdom, right there.

On the mango-colored accent wall next to the open kitchen those essential ingredients are on display. But as aesthetically pleasing as those spice-laden bottles are, they aren't just for looks: The rows of tall, wide-mouthed glass Ball jars house the building blocks to many of our

dishes. They get a workout every week and frequently need refilling.

One jar contains green cardamom pods; take a whiff inside that lid for a cool, fresh scent. In contrast, the neighboring larger black cardamom pods have this intense earthy, smoky smell and flavor. Tiny cumin seeds, which we use liberally at JBC, pack a pungent nuttiness that defies their size. And the similarly shaped but slightly larger green fennel seeds boast a licorice hit. Meanwhile, yellowish-brown fenugreek seeds, which resemble little pebbles, add an astringent, bitter taste and quintessential "curry-like" smell to dishes.

Also in the lineup: Gold-colored coriander seeds offer their citrus-like scent. The pungency embedded in brown and yellow mustard seeds is only

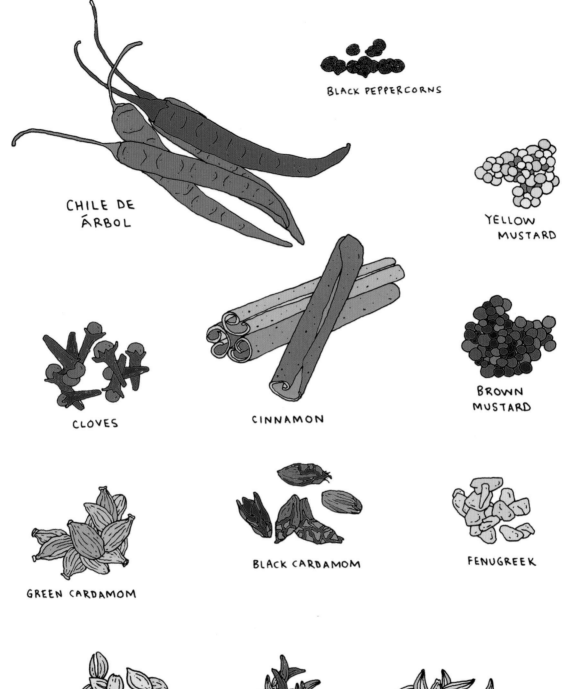

BLACK PEPPERCORNS

CHILE DE
ÁRBOL

YELLOW
MUSTARD

CLOVES

CINNAMON

BROWN
MUSTARD

GREEN CARDAMOM

BLACK CARDAMOM

FENUGREEK

CORIANDER

CUMIN

FENNEL

apparent upon cooking, when they pop and release their flavor kick. Cassia, bark-like cinnamon sticks, offer a hint of bitterness with cinnamon's signature sweetness. And spiky little cloves exude a sweet, unique fragrance and flavor that some associate with winter holidays, though they are a staple in our kitchen year-round. Credit black peppercorns and dried chiles for providing serious heat in our spice blends. My favorite flavor bomb: chile de árbol. These small, skinny, long, and bright red chiles offer bold in-your-face heat. They kick up the seasoning accent of sauces, curries, and soups in a JBC kind of way.

There are a few spices we buy already ground, such as chili powder and turmeric, as we're able to source high-quality superfine versions locally. We also buy pre-ground *amchur* (*amchoor*), also known as green or unripe mango powder. This pale tan powder adds a warm, fruity scent and an acidic, tart taste to any masala. Of course we use a lot of turmeric, a current darling of hippies and hipsters for its anti-inflammatory properties and health benefits. It's a staple in Indian cooking for its musty, earthy, slightly bitter flavor and its bright yellow to orange hue.

There's space on the spice rack for something else I'm rather fond of: Indian black salt—which, heads-up, isn't actually black: after it's ground, it's a silvery pink! We buy that already ground, too. There's no confusing its odor: black salt is a Himalayan volcanic salt that has a strong sulfurous smell (pretty much just like rotten eggs), so a little goes a long way. The salt is an essential ingredient in many savory snacks, street foods, and drinks, like our Nimbu Pani, a cilantro lemonade with toasted cumin.

That's more than a dozen flavor accents right there! And we use them every day.

We roast all our own masalas or spice blends at JBC. There's something soothingly familiar about spreading out spices in a single layer on a rimmed baking sheet. I like the feel of the different shapes and sizes of the spices under my hand, it's like a palette full of potential. Toasting spices brings out their inherent flavor and fragrance.

Cooking is all about balance; I'm always looking for that in a dish. How do the sweet, savory, salty, sour, spicy, bitter, acidic elements align? You're looking for that balance in a spice blend, too. Heat, floral notes, nuttiness, earthiness, smokiness, piquant punchiness—all of

it—because you're layering on so much flavor that way.

||||||||||||||||||||||||||||||

For the first twelve to eighteen months after Juhu Beach Club opened, I spent what I called Masala Mondays—the one day of the week the restaurant is closed—making all of our spice blends for the week ahead. Since masalas are at the heart of our menu, that wasn't a job I was willing to delegate until I knew my kitchen crew was up to the task. Besides, I enjoy the meditative process of making masalas. Some of the recipes we use are fairly traditional—such as JBC Garam Masala and Chai Masala— with modest tweaks or modern riffs on standard spice blends. Others—like the smoky black cardamom masala—are all my own invention.

I fell in love with black cardamom about ten years ago, about the same time I had my spice epiphany. The flavor is so different from the food I grew up with—my mother rarely cooked with black cardamom, it's more of a Northern India thing. I'm drawn to the rich, smoky flavor these big black oval pods impart and their woody fragrance. The spice pairs brilliantly with the rustic, slow-cooked meats I'm fond of preparing, like braised short rib or lamb shank curry, with the meat falling off the bone. It's the spice blend used on the Holy Cow Pav, which was a huge hit at my pop-up, the most popular sandwich in the bunch. I credit the masala for that.

As much as I thrive expediting at the counter or working the line, there's a kind of melancholy I enjoy when I'm alone in the kitchen making masalas. I listen to music—some chill emo, R&B, a little Drake. I simultaneously zone out and focus on the task in front of me. I like the precision of measuring the spices, the smell of them toasting. The act of setting up for the week ahead appeals to my get-shit-done personality, and I still derive a great deal of pleasure knowing that our diners are going to enjoy the flavors here—the masalas are really the backbone of the restaurant's menu. They're what make our dishes distinct.

DHANNA JEERU MASALA

Makes 1 cup

¾ cup coriander seeds
¼ cup cumin seeds

In Gujarati *dhanna jeeru* literally means "coriander cumin," and that's exactly what this is. A staple in Gujarati cooking found in many dishes, it's one of the few blends that we don't toast before grinding.

Combine the spices and grind them in a spice grinder in batches, until all spices are fully ground. Mix well and keep in an airtight container for up to 4 weeks.

MUSTARD FENUGREEK MASALA

Makes 1 cup

3 tablespoons coriander seeds
1 tablespoon cumin seeds
1 black cardamom pod
1 teaspoon fenugreek seeds
1 teaspoon cloves
½ stick cinnamon
½ teaspoon brown mustard seeds
½ cup dried chile de árbol
1 teaspoon whole black
   peppercorns

This masala was originally created for a poultry marinade at JBC. Since then, the spicy, tangy, bitter, and bright masala has crept into a variety of dishes on the menu. It makes a great rub for chicken, firm whitefish, or lighter vegetables like zucchini, asparagus, and cauliflower.

Preheat the oven to 350° F. Measure out all the spices onto a sheet pan. Place the pan in the oven for 5 to 7 minutes until the spices begin to slightly smoke and turn a little brown. Remove the pan from the oven and set aside to cool. When the spices are fully cooled, grind them in a spice grinder in batches, until all spices are completely ground. Mix them well and keep in an airtight container for up to 4 weeks.

JBC GARAM MASALA

Makes 2 cups

½ cup coriander seeds
¼ cup cumin seeds
¼ cup fennel seeds
1 tablespoon green cardamom pods
10 black cardamom pods
1 tablespoon cloves
2 2-inch cinnamon sticks
½ cup dried chile de árbol
¼ cup black peppercorns

Garam masala is probably one of the most well-known Indian spice blends, which is why you can find it in most American grocery stores. But don't buy it. Homemade garam masala is so much more flavorful. Every cook or kitchen in India has its own garam masala recipe. In Hindi, *garam* means warm or hot, not to be confused with spicy. This masala is intended to fuse together a blend that is warming but not overly spicy.

For recipe method, see Mustard Fenugreek Masala, page 102.

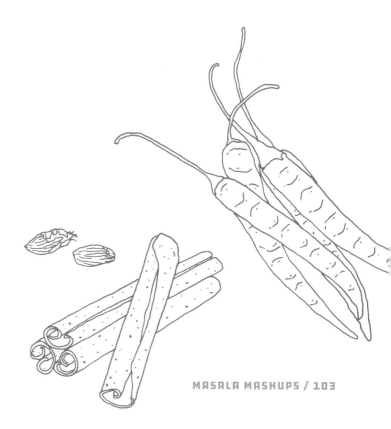

SMOKY BLACK CARDAMOM MASALA

Makes 2 cups

¼ cup coriander seeds

2 tablespoons cumin seeds

½ cup fennel seeds

¼ teaspoon green cardamom pods

10 black cardamom pods

1 teaspoon cloves

1 2-inch cinnamon stick

⅓ cup black peppercorns

This was one of the first masalas I created on my own. I wanted something that would pair well with dark red meats and slow-cooked sauces. Black cardamom is dried over hot coals which imparts an intensely smoky aroma to it—one that seemed a perfect match for a meat cut like beef short ribs or a lamb shank. I thought fennel seeds would be the perfect sweet balance for the black cardamom. In addition to slow braises, I recommend this masala as a dry rub for beef or lamb that's going on the grill.

For recipe method, see Mustard Fenugreek Masala, page 102.

SLOPPY P MASALA

Makes 2 cups

¾ cup coriander seeds

⅓ cup cumin seeds

1 tablespoon fennel seeds

½ teaspoon green cardamom pods

1 tablespoon fenugreek seeds

½ teaspoon cloves

⅓ cup black peppercorns

1½ tablespoons Indian red chili powder

1½ tablespoons amchoor
   (dried mango powder)

1 tablespoon black salt

This masala really packs a punch, which is how it transforms all of the mild minced vegetables in the Sloppy Lil' P Pav into something magically mouthwatering. It's also the base for our house chaat masala.

Preheat the oven to 350° F. Place the whole spices onto a sheet pan. Put the pan in the oven for 5 to 7 minutes until the spices begin to smoke slightly and turn a little brown. Remove the spices from the oven and set them aside to cool. Place the powdered spices in a bowl. When the whole spices are fully cooled, grind them in batches. Mix them well with the powdered spices and keep in an airtight container for up to 4 weeks.

CHAAT MASALA

Makes 1 cup

¾ cup Sloppy P Masala
   (see recipe page 104)
¼ cup Indian red chili powder

Every street cart in India has its own blend of chaat masala. Ours is essentially an amped-up version of our Sloppy P Masala. We use chaat masala in so many different ways because it is so versatile. It adds liveliness to sautéed vegetables, French fries, in sandwiches, and in compound butter.

Mix well with ground spices and keep in an airtight container for up to 4 weeks.

KHEEMA MASALA

Makes 2 cups

½ cup coriander seeds
¼ cup cumin seeds
⅓ cup fennel seeds
1½ tablespoons green cardamom pods
7 black cardamom pods
1 teaspoon fenugreek seeds
1 teaspoon cloves
1 tablespoon black peppercorns
1 teaspoon amchoor (dried mango
   powder)
1 teaspoon black salt

Kheema, a ground lamb or beef sloppy joe, is one of my go-to street food dishes. But since I grew up in a mainly vegetarian household, it wasn't until I reached adulthood that I discovered this meaty Indian pav and its flavorful masala. It's a perfect marriage of the bright tang of our chaat masala, mixed with earthy spices like fennel and cardamom, which pair so well with red meats. Sprinkle a little of this masala in a burger patty or rub on a lamb chop.

For recipe method, see Sloppy P Masala, page 104.

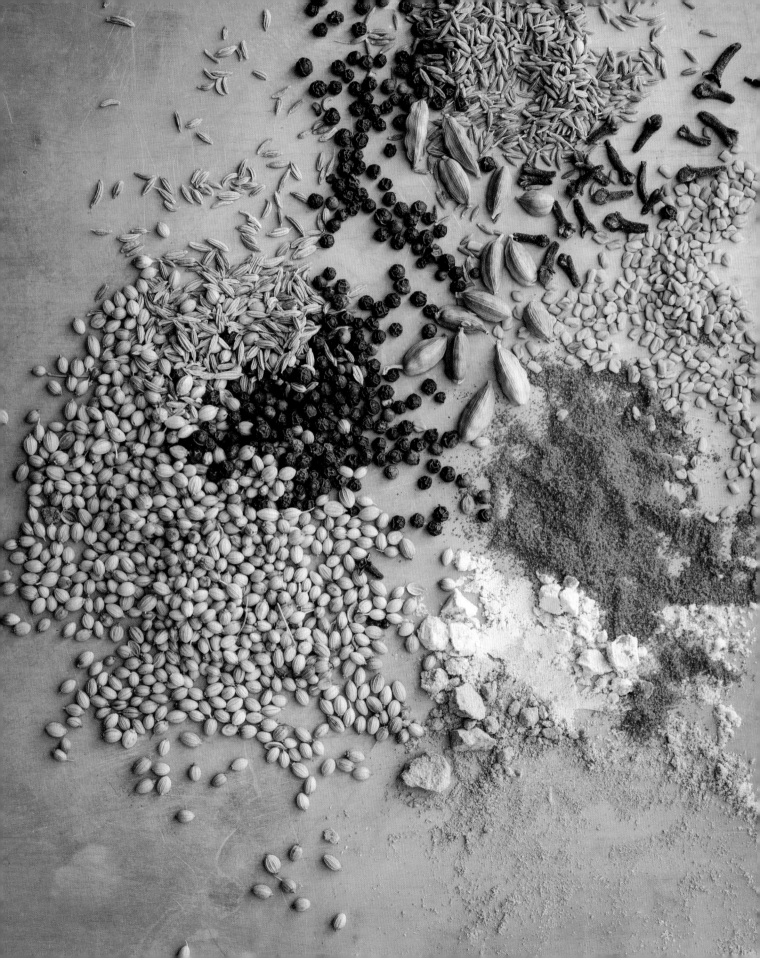

SAMBAR MASALA

Makes 2 cups

¾ cup coriander seeds

1 tablespoon cumin seeds

½ teaspoon fenugreek seeds

1½ cups dried red chile de árbol

1 tablespoon black peppercorns

1½ tablespoons chana dal
  (a dark yellow lentil)

1½ tablespoons washed urad dal
  (a white lentil)

1½ tablespoons toor dal
  (a bright yellow lentil)

1 tablespoon turmeric powder

This masala provides the bulk of the kicky flavor in our Sambar, a South Indian lentil soup we serve at brunch with our doswaffle. Like the chutney masala, which also has roots in Southern India, this masala has dried lentils in addition to whole spices that are roasted and ground together. It's a terrific addition to vegetable sautés and seafood dishes such as calamari or mussels.

For recipe method, see Sloppy P Masala, page 104. Treat the lentils like whole spices.

CHUTNEY MASALA

Makes 1 cup

2 teaspoons fenugreek seeds

2 teaspoons brown mustard seeds

4 dried chile de árbol

4 tablespoons chana dal
  (a dark yellow lentil)

2 tablespoons washed urad dal
  (a white lentil)

This masala is used in our coconut chutney and combines pungent spices, chiles, and dried lentils. The mustard and fenugreek give the blend a bitter tang, the red chiles bring the heat, and the lentils add an earthy flavor and transform the texture.

For recipe method, see Mustard Fenugreek Masala, page 102. Treat the dal as you would whole spices.

CURRY POWDER

Makes 1 cup

½ cup coriander seeds

¼ cup cumin seeds

½ tablespoon fenugreek seeds

½ tablespoon cloves

½ tablespoon brown mustard seeds

½ tablespoon yellow mustard seeds

5 dried chile de árbol

½ tablespoon black peppercorns

½ tablespoon turmeric powder

I had never heard of "curry powder" growing up. It doesn't really exist in an Indian kitchen. I do like the underlying flavor profile of the Madras or other grocery store blends, though, so I set out to make our own version in-house. Use this blend in any recipe that calls for curry powder.

For recipe method, see Sloppy P Masala, page 104.

CHAI MASALA

Makes 1 cup

½ cup green cardamom pods
¼ cup cloves
5 2-inch cinnamon sticks
¼ cup black peppercorns

Trust me: this masala makes a chai that is better than any at the corner coffee shop. We also use this masala to add a sweet note to candied pecans, and it is a welcome addition to a rich duck dish or sweet vegetables like fall squash.

For recipe method, see Mustard Fenugreek Masala, page 102.

PICKLE MASALA

Makes 1 cup

¼ cup fenugreek seeds
½ cup brown mustard seeds
¼ cup black peppercorns
1 tablespoon turmeric powder
1 tablespoon Indian red chili powder

This masala is the base flavor in our Granny Smith apple pickle. Word to the wise: It is definitely an acquired taste as it's full of bitter and astringent qualities, so a little goes a long way. I recommend pairing it with sweet and tart fruits and vegetables to balance its intensity.

For recipe method, see Sloppy P Masala, page 104.

THE SPICE OF LIFE

Since aromatic spice blends are a cornerstone to everything we do at Juhu Beach Club, I'm serious about where I source spices. We buy most of our spices in bulk from Vik's, a beloved Berkeley institution for more than two decades. Vik's started as a wholesale distributor of ingredients and equipment, selling to Indian groceries and restaurants all over California. Over time, they opened a small grocery and a decidedly "no-frills" street food counter in the front of their original warehouse location. Vik's quickly developed a cult following for its traditional Indian snacks known as chaat. In 2009, Vik's moved to a new, larger warehouse space, not far from its industrial original location. These days, the restaurant can seat a few hundred in its cafeteria-esque space.

Whenever you go there, it's always loud and bustling and packed with people—just like India. And, just as in India, you can watch your order being made: The *cholle bhature*, a big, showy, puffy fried bread, is one of their signature dishes. I always order that—and whatever special the owner, Amod Chopra, wants me to try—when I eat there. I have a good working relationship with Amod and his family. We have a mutual admiration for each other's businesses—and, of course, we appreciate each other's food.

I also go to Oaktown Spice Shop, across from Lake Merritt, in Oakland. It's like an old-time apothecary. Row upon row of herbs and spices from all corners

of the globe in massive jars greet you as you walk in. So does the scent of what's on those shelves; it's a sensory playground in that store. I get ghost peppers from the owner John Beaver. Originally from India, ghost peppers are one of the hottest chile peppers on the planet. We make Ghost Pepper Chutney that goes with our Vada Pav, the JBC version of a deep-fried potato puff slider.

Oaktown has this massive, industrial-size spice grinder. I've used it once or twice when I've needed to grind a large quantity of spices for an event. At the restaurant we use a Vitamix that's designated solely for grinding spices. I suggest home cooks buy a coffee grinder or an inexpensive blender for the same purpose. Since it's tough to get the scent and flavor of spices out of equipment no matter how thoroughly you clean a grinder or blender, it makes sense to have one just for spices. Not everyone wants their coffee tasting like cardamom—or black salt.

It's worth the time and investment to make your own masalas. Freshly ground spices offer an intensity that can't be replicated by a jar of "curry powder"— whatever that is. Whole spices can last a long time (several months to a year) if stored in a cool, dry place. But once those spices are ground, their potency starts to wane. That's why boxed masalas tend to have a homogenous stale flavor.

Just as with meat and vegetable selection, when it comes to spices, fresh really is best. I get it that buying, storing, blending, toasting, and grinding your own spices can feel daunting at first. There are all these different shapes, textures, smells, and tastes to keep track of.

As with any cooking, when you start out it's smart to follow the recipe to the letter for a masala, like the ones in this book. As you become more comfortable with the process and figure out what each spice brings to the mix, you can tweak a masala to suit your own taste. Maybe you like more heat, so you punch up the chile proportions. Or maybe you skip the black salt. Or maybe you cut back on the cinnamon or cardamom to bring down the sweetness.

The #1 key to success in spice shopping: You want to pick a place that has high turnover. Spices that have been hanging around in a store or warehouse for a long time—well, all the flavor and fire gets sapped out of them. Really old spices have a one-note taste or, worse, resemble sawdust. For this reason, I don't recommend buying whole spices from a traditional grocery unless it is a more commonly used spice like black peppercorns, which likely aren't sitting on shelves for too long.

We tend to re-up our masalas once a week in the restaurant. Once ground, our masalas are kept in quart and pint containers. We keep them two weeks tops.

Kitchen truth: Stale spices can ruin a dish. And the opposite is also true: Fresh, fragrant spices can turn a good dish into a great one. So it's worth the effort to find the places in your community that stock quality whole spices. If you can't find a shop close by that sells spices, go online and order from places like Kalustyan's in New York City. (See more about sourcing on page 13.)

PLEASE
PARK & LOCK
We cannot be responsible
for car or contents

ALL PARKING MUST BE
**PAID
IN ADVANCE**
Failure to pay in advance
or properly park will result
in citation

Violators' Cars
Cited or Towed
CALL (510) 655-1345

Moving to Oakland just made sense to me; there is an energy here that's exciting. And it's where my community is.

On a whim, friends suggested that Ann and I check out a house to rent in Oakland. This was in 2011, and by then almost all of our friends were living there. Oakland felt a little rough around the edges, like the Mission District in San Francisco did back in the late '90s when I lived there. People were leaving San Francisco for a lot of reasons: priced out, wanting more space, fed up with the tech invasion by a bunch of mostly white bros.

So we go to look at this house near our friends in a neighborhood called Temescal, in North Oakland. Temescal has a village-like feel; it's the former neighborhood of working-class Italians. Past and present: Temescal has multicultural roots. There's an established restaurant row, and the diversity of the neighborhood is reflected in the restaurants: Korean, Ethiopian, Mexican, Mediterranean. There's an old-school donut shop and a modern ice creamery, longtime dive bars and a new beer garden, as well as a fried chicken sandwich shop run by an Australian American. The Sunday farmers' market is full of families with young kids.

Like other Oakland neighborhoods, the area has a strong art and activist presence. You can see it in the mosaic murals in the neighborhood and in the "Refugees Welcome Here" signs in storefronts. But, no question, the area is gentrifying. The two cute alleys off the main drag—Alley 49 and Temescal Alley—house a bunch of boutique businesses that sell jewelry, jeans, succulents, and herbal elixirs. There's a retro cool barber and a café roasting Third Wave coffee. The neighborhood is bikeable, which matters to me. But there's no grocery shop or hardware store. And the community also has all the typical challenges of an urban neighborhood: crime, homelessness, rising house prices.

The pluses outweigh the minuses in my mind. It's a pretty cool place to live.

We took one look at the three-bedroom Craftsman bungalow from the 1920s for rent in a quiet, residential community—it has a great kitchen and apricot, plum, apple, Asian pear, and orange trees in the backyard—and were sold. Our neighborhood couldn't be more diverse: There's another lesbian couple; across the street from us live a straight African American couple with five boys; there's a Jewish lesbian couple with two biracial kids. Straight, gay, biracial couples, some with kids, some not—it's a mix. We feel like we belong here.

We jumped at the opportunity to move. When people get priced out of a city, it is the people of color, the queers, the artists, and the activists that are pushed out first. Those were "our people," and Oakland seemed to be full of them.

After the deal I was working on to open JBC in San Francisco fell through, I came to see it as a blessing, not a curse. I wanted to open the restaurant in Oakland, my new home. And I found a spot just down the street from our house.

It was a bit off the beaten path—tucked away from Telegraph Avenue—in a little strip mall behind a check-cashing outlet and a pawnshop. The space was already outfitted as a restaurant; we just needed to make it our own.

I feel like Oakland is a place where we can do things. And when I say "we," I mean real people. Not just tech millionaires and trust funders. There's a camaraderie among Oakland business owners and in our industry. It's warm and welcoming. People here represent a range of racial, economic, and sexual orientations.

The town champions independent thinkers, makers, and a DIY ethos.

There's a thriving and growing restaurant scene here—and many of these places are owned and run by women chefs of diverse ethnic backgrounds and culinary traditions. It's kind of a no-brainer: I belong here.

⸺

Ann and I see the restaurant as an extension of our home.

In the summer of 2013, Prop 8, a statewide ballot proposition that eliminated same-sex couples' right to marry, was overturned by the U.S. Supreme Court. That decision paved the way for gay marriages to begin again in California. Everyone in the queer community was elated. We hadn't planned an event; we just said "come celebrate" on social media. It was June 26, 2013, the Friday night of San Francisco Pride weekend. All these people just started showing up with rainbow feather boas and other festive stuff. They were our friends, regulars, and people we didn't even know who wanted to be in community.

You could feel the love in the room. People wanted to be in a place that felt queer. It's funny because every year around Pride all these local restaurants and bars hang rainbow flags in their

divey spots, but that's not my world: our restaurant is a bright, light-filled environment. We have pink walls after all.

My queer friends have toddlers, go to bed at ten, and frequent farmers' markets. We wanted to create community where all kinds of queer and colorful people are comfortable. There's a reason I call the restaurant a mom-and-mom shop. This is a business that Ann and I run together. Sure, I'm the chef, I'm the Indian, but Ann's played an equal role in creating this place: from the interior to the menu to the financial side. Calling our place a mom-and-mom shop is cheeky and subversive. We're taking this traditional idea and making it our own— just like marriage equality.

windows. I get it: it's a show of solidarity. I remember asking Ann, thinking somehow we had screwed up the first year we were open: "Honey, do we need a rainbow flag in the window?" And she looked at me with a sigh and a smile and said: "Honey, you are a walking rainbow flag."

What I loved about that pre-Pride night was just how spontaneous it was. Juhu Beach Club was a place people felt like they wanted to come to. We're not a gay bar. Gay bars are normally dark,

It's Monday, November 7, 2016—the day before the election. I'm lugging chicken, produce, and a bunch of spice bowls to a basement kitchen in Uptown Oakland at Youth Radio's CHEF Program designed to help young people of color learn to cook nutritious food. I've been asked to come teach the cooking class as part of a program run by the nonprofit Cooking Project, founded by Michelin-starred chef Daniel Patterson, who is also the cofounder, along with

Roy Choi, of Loco'l. There's a Loco'l in Uptown and another in Watts; these guys are trying to bring healthy, affordable fast food to low-income people of color in underserved neighborhoods. I'm down with that.

Fluorescent lights, an ancient stove, mismatched kitchen equipment, dull knives. That's the Youth Radio kitchen. No worries, I can work with whatever. As a professional chef, you need to be able to pivot quickly and adjust expectations based on the resources available to you. That's what we do.

Today's recipe is a classic chicken curry; it's on the menu at Juhu. For me it's an opportunity to teach young people, especially low-income students of color going to crappy public schools, how to cook a meal for themselves. A lot of these teenagers have never seen spices in whole form; they are excited to learn and taste and smell. One teenager picks up something and says: "This looks like a stick." I explain it is a stick, a cinnamon stick. He says it smells like Christmas. Everyone in the room learns something that day. That's why I do these classes.

I want to connect with these African American students. And, I hope, just my presence might serve as an inspiration. If I were another tall white guy in a chef's jacket, that's one thing; the kids don't see themselves in him.

When I'm in there, showing them how to marinate chicken or grind spices, it's different for obvious reasons. I'm brown, female, look sort of youthful, wear hoodies, can meet a person in conversation where they're at. Maybe that gives them the feeling they could do this too. The kids don't care if you're "famous." They really don't care. They want to meet someone they can relate to.

After assigning different tasks I move around the room. I demonstrate technique as I go: basic skills like it's easier to chop an onion when you cut it in half, and then lay the flat side on the cutting board. Two girls, with seriously major nail action going on, opt to prep the chicken for the curry. When I work my way to their station, they're randomly hacking that chicken into pieces. It doesn't faze me. I deal with this kind of thing every day in my restaurant. You're always training someone. In this industry you're a teacher every day; that's what we do.

I just say: "Hey, can I show you something?" It's an invitation, whether about how to chop an onion, remove skin from a chicken, cut meat into pieces. There are all these tricks and techniques you learn along the way to do these things efficiently and effectively in a working kitchen. One of my bosses used to say: "Take it or leave it." I really appreciated that. It was like, let me show you a skill, but we're all different, so maybe what works for me doesn't work for you. Still be open to it. That's how I teach, too: Be open, and take it or leave it.

There's a lot for the students to absorb from one recipe in one afternoon: how to make a marinade, how to blend a masala, how to assemble and cook the components of a curry, how to prep and cook sides that pair well with the main dish, including basmati rice tinged with turmeric and a cooling cucumber raita. Cooking rice well is a skill. Juggling the different components of a recipe requires focus. Timing each dish so it's all ready to eat together is an art. It all comes with practice.

The night after class, after the voting booths have closed, I'm tracking the election results as they come in. It's hard to digest the news. As a brown immigrant, I worry about my future here. I also worry about the future of the people I care about who are female, black, Mexican, Muslim, LGBTQ, disabled—in some way considered "other" or "lesser" by the newly elected president and his administration. I'm depressed, sad, frightened, and I'm not alone.

And here's what keeps hope alive for me: The night before those stunning election results were tallied, I'd cooked chicken curry with a group of youth who are fierce, funny, and ready to slay. This is the future I believe in. Shelby Starks, who oversees culinary instruction at Youth Radio, thanked me after the class, and, with a phrase she frequently uses with the students told me "because of you . . . the students trust their dopeness." #TrustYourDopeness. What could be more important for our at-risk youth today?

||||||||||||||||||||||

Hiring a multicultural staff that reflects the community the restaurant resides in is important to me. The kitchen at Juhu Beach Club is like opposite day. We love, appreciate, and champion all kinds of people of different races, ethnicities, socioeconomic backgrounds, sexual orientation, genders.

Diversity is what brings kitchen culture back to the food. As badass as it would be, I don't want a kitchen full of queer Indian women. Anytime one group of people dominates in the kitchen, you

create a culture that's about that and less about the restaurant and its food.

My front-of-house staff embody my dining room philosophy. It's so important to me that everybody who walks in here gets treated fairly. My servers know we need to go above and beyond for a lot of our customers who are people of color, women, differently gendered, because those are the folks that are used to being treated like shit. I'm telling you firsthand: it happens all day long and every day, and it's something I take very seriously.

It's not about how many people of color or women you hire—it's about how many you *retain*. How many of them actually stick around? Are you actually invested in creating an environment they want to be in? That is where the disconnect is in the industry. It's like, "How do we fix this?" We don't just fix things by not hiring the white guy and hiring the black lady. That's not how I created the environment I have at Juhu. I hire a lot of different people, and I don't have prejudices about how a person will perform based on how he/she/they look/s. I assess their character and whether they show respect to me as the owner. And then I go with my gut.

JBC DOSWAFFLE

Makes 6 to 8 doswaffles

1 cup washed urad dal
  (a white lentil)
¼ teaspoon fenugreek seeds
3 cups idli rice (available in most
  Indian grocery stores)
salt to taste
1 cup Ghee (see recipe
  page 22)
Masala Potatoes
  (see recipe, page 125)
Sambar (see recipe, page 128)
Coconut Chutney (see recipe,
  page 127)

The *doswaffle* (pronounced *doe-swah-full*): n. Juhu Beach Club's creation, a hybrid of a South Indian dosa with a Belgian-style waffle and a brunch staple at the restaurant. The gluten-free batter is made from rice and lentils that are soaked, ground, and then naturally fermented—just as is traditional dosa batter—for at least six hours or preferably overnight. The idea came to me while staring at waffle irons in a restaurant supply store. We chefs find our inspiration in all kinds of settings. My doswaffle has all the components found in a classic *masala dosa*, but slightly reinterpreted. And it requires some advance planning: the batter needs to sit for 2 to 3 days prior to use to double in size.

To soak the rice and lentils:

Rinse and drain the urad dal in cold water 3 to 4 times. Fill a container of rinsed dal with cold water, so the water is about 2 inches above the dal. Stir in the fenugreek seeds. Cover and let sit at room temperature overnight (or at least 6 hours).

Repeat the same process for the rice, leaving out the fenugreek seeds.

To grind the batter:

In batches in a blender, grind the dal, making sure there is enough liquid (covering about 1 inch above the dal). Grind the dal twice, scraping down the sides of the blender between batches, then pour the puréed dal into a large plastic container. The consistency of the puréed dal should be smooth, fluffy, and creamy—similar to that of a milk shake. Set aside.

Next grind the rice in batches in the blender with its soaking water. Rice is harder to grind but also retains more moisture, so take care not to add too much water—no more than an inch above the solids.

(recipe continues)

The puréed rice will be a bit thinner than the dal and slightly grainy like semolina, but shouldn't be watery.

After both the dal and rice are ground, mix them together with a spatula. Continue to mix with your hands: This is an important step as the natural oils on your skin help to kickstart fermentation.

To ferment:
Leave the batter in a warm, dark place in a covered container large enough for the batter to double in size. The batter should sit for 24 to 36 hours and rise significantly in that time. If there are no signs of rising after 12 hours, look for a warmer spot for the container. Options include inside a gas oven with the pilot lit, in an oven with a "proofing" temperature (under 120°F), a laundry room, or next to a heater.

Making the doswaffles:
Following fermentation, vigorously mix the batter with a whisk to make sure it is smooth and there are no solids on the bottom of the container. Season the batter with salt to taste. Heat a waffle maker to the high setting. Most home waffle makers beep when they are ready to use. Brush the top and bottom of the waffle maker with ghee and pour in the batter. Close the lid and don't open it again for at least 5 minutes—the batter should be set before you open the machine. After 5 minutes, take a peek and check on the doswaffle. The waffle should have a lightly browned crispy exterior and a soft and pillowy interior.

Serve with masala potatoes, sambar, and coconut chutney.

MASALA POTATOES

Serves 4-6

4 pounds red potatoes,
  washed and diced into
  bite-size pieces
2 tablespoons neutral oil
½ cup fresh curry leaves
1 tablespoon brown mustard seeds
1 cup red onions, julienned
1 teaspoon turmeric powder
1 teaspoon Indian red chili powder
2 pinches salt

Like American home fries, these potatoes are a simple yet supremely satisfying combination. Masala Potatoes promise a balance of sweetness from caramelized onions, heat from spices, and crispy-on-the-outside-soft-on-the-inside potato. The potatoes are a natural side dish with a doswaffle, and also pair well with a traditional American-style egg and toast breakfast.

Place the potatoes in a stockpot, cover them with cold water, and add a pinch of salt. Bring the water to a boil and simmer until the potatoes are cooked through and easy to pierce with a small knife—at least 15 minutes. Drain the potatoes in a colander and set aside.

Heat a sauté pan on high and add the oil. When the oil is hot, add the curry leaves and mustard seeds. A note of caution: they will pop and sizzle. Once the sizzling slightly subsides—after about 1 minute—add the onions and season with salt. Stir the onions until they soften and start to brown on the edges—about 5 to 10 minutes. Add the cooked potatoes and season with the turmeric and chili powder. Continue cooking and stirring until the potatoes brown on both sides—roughly 10 minutes. Taste and add more salt if needed.

COCONUT CHUTNEY

Makes 1 quart

½ cup ginger, minced

½ cup serrano chiles, minced

2 cups whole plain yogurt

1 cup roughly chopped cilantro leaves

1 tablespoon salt

2 cups fresh grated coconut

2 tablespoons Chutney Masala
  (see recipe page 110)

¼ cup neutral oil

½ cup fresh curry leaves

½ tablespoon brown mustard seeds

The first time I made this recipe, with my mother's guidance, I was blown away by its distinctive flavor. The technique of tempering or adding aromatics—in the case of this recipe, curry leaves and mustard—in hot oil is a common practice in many Indian dishes, especially in South India where this chutney's origins lie.

In a blender purée the ginger, chiles, yogurt, cilantro leaves, and salt. Add the coconut, chutney masala, and ¼ cup of water. Purée until smooth-ish: this chutney has a slightly grainy texture. Set aside the purée in a metal bowl. Heat the oil in a sauté pan on high. When the oil begins to smoke, add the curry leaves and mustard seeds: use caution as they will sizzle and pop. After about 30 seconds remove the leaves and seeds from the heat and pour into the chutney. Use a spoon and quickly stir in the sizzling oil so it completely mixes in the chutney. Taste and add more salt if needed.

SAMBAR

Makes 3 quarts

2 cups toor dal (available at
   Indian markets)

2 cups okra, cut into half moons

1 teaspoon salt

1 teaspoon neutral oil (for okra)

¼ cup neutral oil (for frying aromatics)

1 dried red chile de árbol

1 teaspoon brown mustard seeds

½ teaspoon fenugreek seeds

10 curry leaves

½ yellow onion, julienned

2 tablespoons Sambar Masala
   (see recipe page 109)

½ teaspoon turmeric powder

1 teaspoon Tamarind Paste
   (see recipe page 23)

2 cups diced butternut squash

2 cups dark greens (such as chard,
   amaranth, or beet greens)

Sambar is a South Indian lentil soup made from toor dal. These yellowish, round, and split lentils cook fairly quickly, which makes this soup a good choice when you are pressed for time. Many different veggies work well in sambar; I like adding okra because something about this soup reminds me of a Creole gumbo. It is also a very spicy and tart soup, so the butternut squash adds an excellent sweet element to balance the flavors. A meal on its own, sambar is traditionally served with dosas or idlis. At the restaurant we serve the soup with a doswaffle.

Rinse the dal under cold water and drain; repeat 3 times. Soak the rinsed dal in a bowl in warm water to cover for about 30 minutes. Transfer the dal and water to a stockpot, and add water to fully cover the dal by at least 2 inches. Season with 2 pinches of salt. Place the stockpot on high heat and bring the water to a boil. When the water is boiling, reduce heat and simmer for about 30 minutes until the dal is soft and beginning to dissolve. Remove the cooked dal from the heat and purée with an immersion blender or let it cool slightly and purée in a traditional blender in batches.

Preheat the oven to 350°F. Toss the okra with the salt and oil. Spread the okra on a baking sheet and roast in the oven for about 10 minutes to soften. Let the okra cool on the baking sheet for about 15 minutes.

Heat a large stockpot on high with the oil and spices. When the spices begin to brown, about 1 minute, add the curry leaves and onion and season with a pinch of salt. After about 3 minutes—when the onions start to soften—add the masala and turmeric. Season with two pinches of salt. Stir to incorporate the spices, about 3 minutes. Pour in the puréed dal and stir to combine. Add the tamarind paste and 1 cup of water. Then add the okra, squash, and greens. Bring the mixture to a boil and reduce the heat to simmer for at least 20 minutes. Check the squash for doneness. Taste and season with more salt if needed. Serve.

JBC FRIED CHICKEN & DOSWAFFLE

Makes 6 servings

6 boneless chicken thighs

1 cup Green Chile Turmeric Marinade
  (see recipe page 45)

Doswaffles (see recipe page 123)

2 cups cornstarch

2 tablespoons salt

2 cups whole plain yogurt

1 cup chickpea flour

1 cup rice flour

1 tablespoon Indian red chili powder

2 quarts of oil (for deep-frying)

Black Pepper Butter
  (recipe follows, page 131)

Spicy Syrup (recipe follows,
  page 131)

Our most popular brunch dish, the JBC Fried Chicken & Doswaffle exemplifies diversity—just like Oakland. The doswaffle meshes the technique behind a traditional South Indian dosa batter, in the form of a classic Belgian waffle shape, with that most American of breakfast traditions: marrying sweet and savory flavors on one plate. Fried chicken & waffles, with roots in African American cuisine, is a brunch standard in Oakland. Like many of our marinade recipes, the chicken tastes best when allowed to sit for at least six hours.

Marinate the chicken thighs in Green Chile Turmeric Marinade and 1 tablespoon salt for at least 6 hours, or ideally overnight.

Prior to cooking chicken, prepare the Doswaffle (see recipe, page 123) and keep warm in a low oven.

To make chicken batter:

Season the cornstarch with 1 tablespoon of salt and set it aside in a medium bowl. In a separate medium bowl mix the yogurt and 1 cup of water with a whisk. Mix together the chickpea flour, rice flour, chili powder, and remaining tablespoon of salt in another medium bowl. Dredge or coat each piece of marinated chicken in the cornstarch first, shaking off any excess. Then dip the chicken pieces in the yogurt mixture, and finally dip the chicken thighs into the flour mixture and set them aside on a sheet pan.

(recipe continues)

Heat the oil for frying to 300°F in a heavy-bottomed, large sauce-pan. Use a thermometer to check the temperature. When all 6 chicken pieces have been dredged, begin frying each piece one by one in the heated oil. Remove the chicken from the heat when the coating begins to crisp and brown—about 5 minutes. Set the chicken aside until ready to serve, no more than 30 minutes. Right before serving, increase the oil heat slightly until the thermometer reaches 350°F and fry each piece of chicken for about 2 minutes. The chicken should be crispy on the outside and cooked through in the center. If you are unsure of the chicken's doneness, poke it in a thick part with a sharp paring knife. The juices that release should be clear not pink; if they are not clear, drop the chicken back into the oil for another 2 minutes.

Garnish the doswaffles with sliced rounds of black pepper butter. Top with crispy fried chicken, and serve with spicy syrup on the side.

Black Pepper Butter

Makes 1 cup

1 cup unsalted butter
2 teaspoons freshly ground
  black pepper
1 teaspoon flaky sea salt
  (we use Maldon)

Cut the butter into 4 pieces and set it in a small glass bowl to soften in a warm place for about 15 to 20 minutes. Once it is softened, place the butter in the bowl of an electric mixer with the paddle attachment, and begin beating the butter on medium speed. Add the pepper and salt and beat again until the seasoned butter is smooth and fluffy.

Spread two layers of plastic wrap on a countertop, stretched out about a foot across. Pour the seasoned softened butter onto the plastic and roll it into a log. Tie each end and chill the log for at least 3 hours in the refrigerator, until the butter is fully chilled in the center. Cut rounds of the butter to garnish the doswaffle.

Spicy Syrup

Makes 1 cup

2 cups pancake syrup
  (we use Log Cabin)
2 teaspoons Indian red chili powder

Heat the syrup and chili powder in a small saucepan on medium heat, until the syrup comes to a simmer—about 10 minutes. Whisk the mixture to remove any excess chili powder lumps. Remove from heat and cool.

CROQUE MEMSAHIB

Makes 6 servings

6 slices white bread
  (we use Pullman loaf)
¼ cup serrano chiles, minced
3 cups Monterey Jack cheese, grated
12 strips Chai-Spiced Bacon
  (see recipe page 136)
2 tablespoons neutral oil
1 dozen eggs
1 cup Tamarind Ketchup
  (see recipe page 207)

Oakland has a strong brunch game. That's where my Indian-inspired *croque*, based on the classic French dish *croque madame*, comes into play. I knew my brunch menu needed to feature eggs and bread in a compelling way. The Hindi word *memsahib* was a title of respect given to white women or women of high social standing during Britain's colonial rule of India. As a child, I generally heard the term being used in a tongue-in-cheek way among Indians: piling on the respect in an ironic fashion. Naming rights aside, this recipe hits all the best brunch notes: spicy, cheesy, carb-y, eggy, bacon-y joy on a plate.

Heat a broiler to high. Place the slices of bread on a sheet pan and top each slice with 1 teaspoon of the chile. Then cover each slice with grated cheese. Lay two bacon slices on top of the cheese in an *X*, and place the sheet pan under the broiler for about 3 to 5 minutes, until the cheese is fully melted.

Heat a nonstick skillet on medium with ½ tablespoon of oil. Fry the eggs in batches—sunny-side up—to desired doneness. Add more oil as needed between the egg batches. Top each cheese-covered toast with two fried eggs. Serve with the tamarind ketchup.

BLACK DAL

Makes 4 quarts

½ cup black chickpeas

1 cup black urad dal

2 tablespoons unsalted butter

½ yellow onion, julienned

2 tablespoons salt

2 tablespoons ginger, minced

2 tablespoons serrano chile, minced

1 tablespoon garlic, minced

2 tablespoons JBC Garam Masala
  (see recipe page 103)

½ cup tomato paste

Yogurt, for serving

1 cup roughly chopped cilantro

This restaurant menu item was a happy accident: a way to use up erroneously delivered lentils we had stored in the pantry. Soup seemed an obvious solution: So I soaked some dal overnight. The next day, as I stirred the pot of rich, black, warm soup, my mind drifted—in a word association way—from black dal to Black Lives Matter. Since then we have given one dollar from every bowl of soup to the movement. This dish makes a satisfying lunch or dinner on a regular rotation.

Rinse the black chickpeas and dal separately and soak them in cold water at room temperature for 10 hours, or ideally overnight.

Melt the butter in a medium stockpot on medium heat. Add the onions, season with some salt, and stir until the onions begin to soften—about 3 minutes. When the onions become soft and translucent, add the ginger, chile, garlic, more salt, and continue to stir to incorporate. After about 3 minutes, add the masala and tomato paste, and stir vigorously to fold this into the onion mixture. Then add 4 cups of water, and use the liquid to scrape any spices from the bottom of the pot.

Pour in the drained dal and chickpeas, and turn the heat up to high. Water should cover at least 1 inch above the pulses; add a little extra if needed.

When the liquid comes to a boil, reduce the heat to low, and let things simmer until the lentils and chickpeas are soft—about 30 to 45 minutes. Season the soup with salt and set aside to cool slightly. After the soup cools, use an immersion blender to purée. The soup can also be puréed in batches in a traditional blender.

Adjust the seasoning, as desired. Serve with a drizzle of yogurt and a sprinkling of cilantro.

SOLIDARITY SOUP

The slogan that morphed into a powerful political movement, Black Lives Matter, was coined in 2013 after African American teen Trayvon Martin's killer, George Zimmerman, was acquitted for his crime. Credit for inspiring the slogan goes to Oakland's Alicia Garza, who posted on Facebook following the verdict: "Black people. I love you. I love us. Our lives matter. Black Lives Matter."

Her sister in political activism Patrisse Cullors crafted a hashtag to accompany the phrase, and the rest is history. The national Black Lives Matter movement has been spurred by the deaths of black and brown people at the hands of police and by the shocking racial disparities within the U.S. criminal justice system. Oscar Grant. Michael Brown. Eric Garner. It's a sad and sorry long list of black people killed by white cops.

Garza, who self-identifies as a queer woman, is of African American and Mexican American heritage and married to a biracial trans man. The first time she came into JBC was for a combined birthday brunch with her partner.

I'm a fan. I wanted to do something concrete in support. As serendipity would have it, we were sent an order of black urad lentils by mistake. They'd been hanging around the restaurant for a while, waiting for me to come up with something creative to do with them. One day it just came to me: I'll make black dal, solidarity soup, and donate a buck a bowl to Black Lives Matter. That's how black dal with a yogurt drizzle and

turmeric oil landed on the JBC menu. It's a small gesture, we're still small business owners, but every bit counts.

Oakland has a strong history of activism from the Black Panther Party to the Occupy movement and now Black Lives Matter and the BlackOUT Collective.

When catastrophic events happen—the things that spark movements like Black Lives Matter, or repealing Prop 8, or resistance in the face of postelection blues—there's a certain sort of aimlessness that we often feel. We don't know what to do, or where to go, or how to be in the world.

I feel this way as much as anyone. And then pretty soon, something else kicks in: First and foremost I can feed people. That's always my go-to when something bad happens. I'm not going to go march down the street anymore; I've done that. I've got a restaurant to run. But what can I do? People have to eat. And I can feed them. And if that's what Juhu Beach Club can offer people, while making them feel safe, at home, in community and raising a little money on the side, that's how we can help.

CHAI-SPICED BACON

Makes 4 servings

1 cup light brown sugar, packed
2 tablespoons Chai Masala
  (see recipe page 111)
12 slices smoked bacon

I can eat this bacon at any time of day, but it is a natural side for breakfast or brunch. We use an applewood-smoked bacon made from heritage breed pork; it has the right amount of smokiness to pair with intense spices.

Combine the sugar and chai masala in a medium bowl. Toss each strip of bacon in the mixture to coat, and then lay them on a sheet pan. Cook the bacon in a 350°F oven for about 10 minutes—until the bacon is browned and rendered of excess fat. Drain each slice on paper towels, and then serve.

HAKKA NOODLES

Makes 4 to 6 servings

4 cups soy sauce (we use low-sodium, Kikkoman brand)

4 cups light brown sugar, packed

1 stalk lemongrass

5 tablespoons ginger, minced

3 garlic cloves, roughly smashed

3 mandarins or tangerines

2 star anise

2 dried red chiles

2 teaspoons black peppercorns

½ cinnamon stick

2 pounds fresh Chinese egg noodles

1 pound ground pork

2 teaspoons Toasted Cumin (see recipe page 25)

½ bunch cilantro, roughly chopped

2 tablespoons neutral oil

1 cup napa cabbage, julienned

1 cup red bell pepper, julienned

1 cup mushrooms (we use brown crimini, shiitake, and matsutake)

1 tablespoon cornstarch

1 bunch scallions, thinly sliced on the bias

Hakka Noodles are one of a few JBC menu items with a Chinese influence. Hakka are an ethnically Chinese nomadic people—originally from the southeastern part of the country—who have reimagined traditional dishes as they've settled in different parts of the world. This dish is a nod to typical Hakka Indian fare. Find fresh egg noodles in Chinese grocery stores; we source ours in Oakland's Chinatown. If fresh noodles aren't an option, I recommend frozen noodles over dried ones.

To make the sauce:

Heat the soy sauce and brown sugar in a stockpot with 2 cups of water on high heat. Whisk to ensure the sugar dissolves. After the sauce comes to a boil, reduce temperature to low and simmer. Peel the outer leaves off the lemongrass, and smash the stalk with the back of a knife to release the flavor. Add the lemongrass, 3 tablespoons ginger, and garlic to the stockpot. Remove the peel from the mandarins and use a sharp knife to remove the extra white pith from the fruit. Juice the mandarins by hand over a sieve to avoid any excess pith. Add the trimmed peels and juice to the soy sauce mixture simmering in the stock-pot. Toast the star anise, chiles, peppercorns, and cinnamon in a small sauté pan on high heat. When the spices begin to smoke, immediately add them to the sauce. Simmer the sauce for about 1 hour on low heat—or until it reduces by about ¼ of the liquid. Strain the solids through a sieve and set aside the sauce.

To cook the noodles:

Heat a large stockpot full of water and a pinch of salt on high. When the water boils, add the noodles and cook according to the packaging. Fresh noodles should take about 3 to 5 minutes. Drain the noodles and toss them with 1 tablespoon of oil to prevent sticking.

(recipe continues)

To prepare the pork:

Mix the ground pork with 2 tablespoons of ginger, cumin, and cilantro. Season with salt and cook a small piece and check to make sure the seasoning is to taste. Heat a sauté pan on medium, add the pork, brown the meat, and cook for about 10 minutes. Drain any excess fat from the pan.

To assemble:

Heat a wok or large sauté pan on high with the oil. When the oil is about to smoke, add the cabbage, peppers, and mushrooms. Stir the vegetables in the pan for about 2 minutes. Then add the pork and noodles and continue sautéing—stirring frequently—for about 2 minutes. Whisk the cornstarch with ¼ cup of water and add this mix to the sauté pan along with 2 cups of the sauce. Shake and stir the pan to fully mix all the ingredients. Cook on high heat for about 3 minutes to let the sauce slightly reduce and thicken. Arrange the noodles on individual plates and top with scallions. Serve immediately.

PORK MOMOS IN JBC KIMCHI BROTH

Makes 4 to 6 servings

1 pound ground pork

1 tablespoon garlic, minced

1 tablespoon ginger, minced

1 teaspoon Toasted Cumin
  (see recipe page 25)

½ bunch of cilantro, roughly chopped

1 egg

24 fresh pot sticker wrappers

½ yellow onion, julienned

3 tablespoons neutral oil

2 cups JBC Kimchi
  (see recipe, page 142)

1 tablespoon red barley miso

2 tablespoons salt

1 bunch bok choy (or other Asian dark
  green), roughly chopped

I first learned about the dumplings known as *momos*, a Nepali specialty, on a trip to Mumbai with Ann. These delicate morsels are influenced by both Chinese and Indian cuisine, as befits a dumpling from Nepal. The momos were so good I was determined to create a JBC version. At the restaurant, we serve them in a broth. These dumplings can be steamed or deep-fried or—in our version—sautéed and then steamed like a pot sticker. This recipe calls for three distinct steps: making the momos, preparing the kimchi, and cooking the dumplings in broth.

Preparing the pork:

Season the ground pork with the garlic, ginger, cumin, and cilantro in a large bowl. Mix thoroughly, add salt. Cook a small piece and taste to check the seasoning; adjust as needed. Then whisk the egg, mix it into the pork, and refrigerate the pork until ready to assemble.

Filling and folding the momos:

Place one fresh wrapper in your left hand. Spoon up a tablespoon of the pork filling and drop it in the middle of the round wrapper. Dip a finger in some water and brush the inside of one half of the wrapper, fold the other side over, and press down to seal. Then wet one corner of the half moon to bring it to meet the other corner and pinch. This creates a tortellini-like shape.

To make the kimchi broth:

In a medium pan, sauté the onion in 1 tablespoon of neutral oil on medium-high heat. Stir the onion as it softens and becomes translucent—about 3 minutes—then add the JBC Kimchi, miso, and 2 cups of water. Increase the heat to high until the water boils, then lower the temperature and simmer for about 15 minutes. Stir occasionally to make sure the miso has fully dissolved into the broth. Taste and add salt if needed.

(recipe continues)

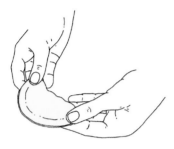

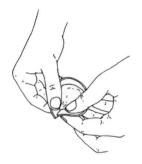

To make the momos:

Heat a large sauté pan on medium high with 2 tablespoons of oil. Place as many momos as will fit in a single layer—flat bottom side down—in the pan. The dumpling skins will begin to brown on the bottom after about 2 minutes, then turn the dumplings to brown the other sides.

If needed, brown the dumplings in batches, wiping the pan with paper towels between batches. To steam the dumplings, add a few ladles of the kimchi broth to 8 browned dumplings in a pan. Bring the broth to a boil, lower the heat, cover, and let the momos steam in the broth for about 3 to 5 minutes, until they are fully cooked in the center. Remove the lid and add a third of the bok choy, and simmer for one or two minutes to slightly reduce the broth. Repeat until all the momos are steamed. Serve them in a bowl.

JBC KIMCHI

Makes 3 quarts

½ cup garlic
½ cup ginger
¼ cup fresh turmeric
½ cup white wine vinegar
½ tablespoon Indian red chili powder
1 teaspoon black salt
½ tablespoon salt
3 quarts napa cabbage,
    julienned

This pickled cabbage is inspired by Korean kimchi. It is by no means traditional to either Korean or Indian cooking, but it's a powerful pickle nonetheless: chock-full of healthful ingredients, such as fresh turmeric and ginger. Aside from the broth for the pork momos, JBC Kimchi adds zest to cheese sandwiches, eggs, fried rice, soup, or salad dressing.

In a food processor combine all the ingredients—except the cabbage—and pulse them until they are all minced. In a large bowl pour the minced mixture over the cabbage and use your hands (with gloves, if preferred) to thoroughly combine. Transfer the mixture to a glass jar or plastic container and refrigerate for at least 24 hours, or ideally 2 days. The pickled cabbage will keep in the refrigerator for at least 3 weeks.

KIDS' BUTTER CHICKEN

*Makes 2 adult and
4 kid servings*

1 pound boneless skinless
  chicken breast
1 lemon, juiced
1 teaspoon salt

For the marinade:
½ cup whole plain yogurt
½ teaspoon turmeric powder
1 teaspoon JBC Garam Masala
  (see recipe page 103)
2 tablespoons neutral oil
½ tablespoon ginger, minced
3 cloves garlic, minced

When Ann and I moved to Oakland, we immediately noticed the number of families with young kids in the area. These days, families with young children are in short supply in many parts of San Francisco. As we planned the menu at JBC, it was clear we would need to appeal to young ones as well as their parents. The JBC Kids' Meal is served in a colorful plastic tiffin, designed by a local artist. The chicken curry is flavorful without being spicy; adults enjoy it too. This dish requires marinating the chicken twice—and for at least three hours the second time around.

Butterfly the chicken by cutting along the long side of the breast, but not all the way through, so that it can be opened up into one larger piece. Marinate the chicken in the lemon juice and salt for at least 30 minutes and no longer than 2 hours.

To make the yogurt marinade:
Fill a traditional blender with the yogurt, turmeric, masala, oil, ginger, and garlic. Blend until the mix is fully puréed.

Remove the chicken from the lemon juice and then marinate it in the yogurt mixture for at least 3 hours and no longer than 24 hours.

(recipe continues)

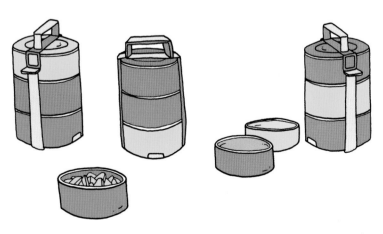

**For the kids' butter
  chicken sauce:**

4 tablespoons unsalted butter

½ tablespoon ginger, minced

3 cloves garlic, minced

1 recipe Kids' Butter Chicken Masala
  (recipe follows, page 145)

1 cup tomato paste

2 cups heavy whipping cream

Turmeric Lemon Rice
  (see recipe page 226)

To make the butter chicken sauce:

Melt the butter in a medium saucepan over medium heat. Add the ginger and garlic along with the kids' butter chicken masala. Stir to keep the spices from sticking to the bottom of the pan. In a measuring cup, combine the tomato paste with 1 cup of water and stir to dissolve the paste. When the aromatics in the saucepan begin to brown, add the tomato paste and stir to release any ingredients stuck to the bottom of the pot. Add the cream and stir continuously to mix all the ingredients thoroughly. Season with salt to taste, and keep stirring every few minutes as the liquid warms. When the sauce is almost boiling, reduce the heat and let it simmer for about 10 minutes.

Butter Chicken:

Heat a grill or broiler to high. Remove the chicken from the marinade and cook on the grill—about 10 minutes per side. Remove from the heat, and cool the meat until its comfortable to touch. Cut the chicken into bite-size pieces and set aside.

To assemble:

Heat the sauce, add the chicken, and simmer. Serve over rice.

Kids' Butter Chicken Masala

Makes ¼ cup

8 green cardamom pods

1 3-inch cinnamon stick

8 cloves

2 black cardamom pods

½ tablespoon fenugreek seeds

Preheat the oven to 350°F. Place all the spices on a sheet pan. Put the pan in the oven for 5 to 7 minutes until the spices begin to turn a little brown. Remove the pan from the oven and set it aside to cool. When it is fully cooled, grind the spices in a spice grinder in batches.

Keep in an airtight container for up to 4 weeks.

GINGER CHILE DUNGENESS CRAB

Serves 2 to 4

½ pound unsalted butter

1 cup fresh curry leaves

¼ cup ginger, minced

¼ cup garlic, minced

1 teaspoon Indian red
  chili powder

¼ cup dry white wine

2 Dungeness crabs, cooked
  and cleaned (substitute other crab or
  lobster if unavailable)

1 tablespoon salt

1 lemon, cut in wedges

½ bunch cilantro, roughly
  chopped

Dungeness crab season is a big deal in the Bay Area. It usually starts right before Thanksgiving and runs until March. The crab is a popular dish on holiday tables—and its limited availability only makes it more special. In my opinion, Dungeness crab rivals New England lobster in terms of taste, texture, and sheer size. A shout-out to my absolute favorite seafood restaurant in Mumbai—Mahesh Lunch Home, where I always order the fresh crab—for seed-planting status on this recipe.

Preheat the oven to 350°F. Melt the butter in a large casserole on medium heat. Add the curry leaves, ginger, and garlic. The curry leaves will crisp, and the ginger and garlic will begin to brown—after about 5 minutes. Then add the chili powder and wine. Let the wine simmer for about 5 minutes, until the alcohol burns off. Break the crab into pieces: snap off the legs and quarter the body using a large chef knife. Add the crab to the butter mixture, season with salt, and toss the crab to coat all the pieces. Place the casserole in the oven for about 15 minutes; halfway through cooking, remove it from the oven and stir to mix the sauce with the crab. Garnish with lemon and cilantro. Serve with crusty bread.

Chapter Five

FARM FRESH

Most Tuesday afternoons and Friday mornings I hop into my mango-colored Mini Cooper and head to local farmers' markets. I've got a little, rusty, secondhand, persimmon-orange-colored dolly, and I'm on a mission. I could send one of my kitchen staff, but it's a chance for me to see, smell, and taste what's ripe right now. I'm a serious fruit and vegetable nerd—it's how I was raised, how I learned to cook professionally, and what I do at the restaurant. Plus, produce is sexy. There's the chance encounter with something unexpected and exciting, along with seasonal inspiration. Whether its tart rhubarb, sweet peaches, or juicy grapes for salads, chaat, chutneys, and pickles, I want to find what shows best and has the most flavor. Same with dark green kales; bright green chicories in all their curly glory; red and golden beets; and Treviso, the beautiful, long purple radicchio that looks almost too perfect to eat. I want it all.

It's no secret that the Bay Area is spoiled for choice when it comes to farmers' markets—between Oakland and Berkeley alone there's a market almost every day of the week. They each have their flavor. I have my favorites.

The Old Oakland farmers' market every Friday morning is arguably the East Bay's most diverse, affordable, and accessible market. It's the People's Market. There are three distinct waves of shoppers here. The early birds—picking through beans and greens when they're barely off the truck—typically older, mostly Asian customers out at the crack of dawn and eager for bargains. These senior shoppers mean business. Trust me, you don't want to get between them and their produce. I give them space. Or to put it more bluntly, I get the fuck out of their way. This is their turf, and I respect elders and people who've forged a path before me. Many of these immigrant shoppers have been coming to this farmers' market—rain or shine, in good times and bad—for two decades or more. This is their market.

And the market caters to them. It's a price-sensitive, decidedly un-bougie place. Many of the vendors are second or third generation farmers and immigrants themselves: Chinese, Thai, Burmese, Laotian, Latino. They may not be certified organic, but they grow food without pesticides and with reverence for the land.

There's whole, live catfish for sale, flopping around on the scales, and a vendor who sells all kinds of eggs—chicken, duck, quail, and the Filipino specialty *balut*. That's a fertilized egg, feathers and all, eaten as a snack throughout Asia. I tried it once—couldn't quite get past the texture. It's an acquired taste.

The market covers several blocks. I make my rounds. Stands are piled high with Asian greens such as *gai lan*, a Chinese broccoli, and *yau choy*, a green-stemmed bok choy. Huge gourds and melons—we're talking door stopper-size—share space with knobby fresh turmeric and galangal, the woody root that looks a bit like ginger but has a citrusy, mustard-like aroma; it's a staple in Thai cooking. Fragrant bunches of herbs such as holy basil (called *tulsi* in Hindi), cilantro, and mint (several varieties of each) are in the mix; stands are well stocked with chiles, too. There are even hardy sticks of purple and beige sugarcane for sale.

It's a city-dwelling cook's dream. People who live close to the market and restaurant folks like me are part of a second shift to comb through the produce stands. Around midmorning, the sun's usually out, and there's a pretty chill vibe. An increasing number of certified organic farmers are popping up here—there's about a dozen now—a reflection of changing demographics and demands. Come lunchtime, the third

wave hits—hungry hordes from nearby businesses storm the prepared food stands and pick up produce in a hurry. I'm long gone.

Old Oakland is a historic district in downtown Oakland that borders the city's Chinatown. The neighborhood boasts charming restored Victorian row houses. Swan's Marketplace, once the area's premium food shopping spot—before it sat vacant for years—has been revamped and reinvigorated. Some of my favorite chefs in town cook here. They all happen to be women. I like to eat at Dominica Rice's Cosecha, Romney (Nani) Steele's The Cook and Her Farmer, and Sarah Kirnon's Miss Ollie's. They serve personal, flavorful, distinctive food: Dominica's reflects her Mexican roots; I'm crazy about her posole verde, and Ann and I order her tamales for the holidays. It's a new tradition we've adopted from Dominica's heritage and a huge hit at gatherings with family and friends. We like to eat at the bar at Nani's California coastal–inspired café; oysters, Prosecco, and one of her salads from Oakland-based farmers make for a relaxed, day-drinking lunch. My go-to at Miss Ollie's is the fried chicken. And I like the Caribbean *phoularie* or split

pea and okra fritters, which are similar to pakoras. My parents lived in Trinidad with my two older sisters before I was born; so I grew up with some island spice at the table. What these women cooks have in common: They're serving comfort food from their culinary traditions and their hearts. These are my kind of people.

The area is gentrifying, like many neighborhoods in Oakland. There's a bunch of bistros and boutiques now. One new restaurant offers a $65 prix fixe tasting menu. Upscale, market-rate condos have sprouted. Still, mainstays of Old Oakland's recent past remain: affordable housing for seniors and low-income residents, graffiti, neighborhood characters.

There's an older African American man, Dale, who shows up on market day with cast-iron pans and Le Creuset cookware he's sourced from estate sales. Ann and I like to collect cookware; we've picked up some choice finds here over the years. He knows what we like by now and sets aside items just for us.

Right before I'm ready to head to the restaurant, I stop by Reem Assil's stand and place a to-go order. Of Palestinian-Syrian background, Reem sells traditional Arab street food made with California love. The dough for her yeasted flatbreads cooks on a traditional convex metal griddle known as a *saj*. The dough puffs up pleasantly and gets a crispy singe on the outside. The bread forms the base for her signature item: a Lebanese street food known as a *man'oushe*—a soft, warm, fluffy, fermented flatbread. The classic is seasoned with a smear of *za'atar*, a savory spice paste made with wild thyme, sumac berry, sesame seeds, olive oil, and salt. My favorite comes with *sujuk* a cured beef sausage; I always ask for hot sauce. They're rolled into a handheld wrap and make an excellent breakfast sandwich. Reem's *muhammara*, roasted red pepper and walnut dip, pairs perfectly with her pillowy, fresh-out-of-the-oven pitas. My staff can't get enough of her breads.

In the summer and fall, this market is my go-to for an impressive array of specialty peppers and fruit. Yerena Farms is a family-owned, organic operation in Watsonville that dates back to 1982, when the farmers, who'd spent years working with their parents for berry giant Driscoll, decided to start their own business. In my opinion, they grow the best strawberries, blackberries, and figs. I make

a beeline for the Borba Farms stand: this third generation farmer—also from Watsonville about 100 miles south of Oakland—produces the most pristine assortment of peppers: Jimmy Nardellos, padrons, habaneros. They come in so many shades: almost black, deep purple, bright red, sunny yellow, vibrant orange, hearty dark green, and pale light green. I want to buy them all.

Tuesday afternoon's Berkeley farmers' market has a different vibe. Almost all the vendors are certified organic. The crowd is a mix of older hippies from around this university town, millennials who live nearby, die-hard farmers' market devotees, and a whole lot of chefs from both the East Bay and San Francisco.

I like the wide range of row crops grown by Full Belly Farm, a 400-acre organic operation in the Capay Valley, north of Sacramento. The farm has been growing produce for 30-plus years. Co-owner Judith Redmond, who is often at the stand, is a well-respected female farm veteran. In addition to produce, Full Belly keeps JBC's flower game strong: I love having flowers I know were grown locally without pesticides in the restaurant.

I stop by Dirty Girl Produce. This Santa Cruz–based farm is known for its dry-farmed Early Girl tomatoes. The waterless growing practice yields a smaller crop and smaller fruit. But what these tomatoes lack in size they make up for in flavor—big time. They are bold, dense, and lush. Try a dry-farmed tomato and you may never eat another kind. They are particularly great for sauces, so come summer these gems go in all our curries. As good as their tomatoes are, I'm all about their hearty bitter greens like radicchio, Treviso, and puntarelle. They're tastier than sweet, delicate salad greens. Their chicories are just gorgeous—so perfectly shaped you don't want to cut them; they're also packed with flavor.

And I swing by the farmstand for Oya Organics, a 15-acre farm in Hollister, not far from Silicon Valley, but a world away. Oya is owned by Marsha Habib and her husband Modesto Sanchez Cruz. The family farm grows a little bit of everything: tomatoes, peppers, corn, beans, squash, lettuces, root crops, dark leafy greens, berries, and melons. I'm all about championing the underdog, the really small or new farm business, the female–owned and operated farm, where the farmer is actually out in the fields picking and also shows up at the market. You build relationships with these farmers over time.

One day Marsha's truck broke down on her way to the market. Even so, she went out of her way to make sure her restaurant clients—including JBC—got what we ordered. She dropped produce on my front porch after midnight. That's dedication. And that kind of personal relationship and commitment from farm to restaurant matters to me. When any of my farmers make it out from under their demanding schedules to come eat at JBC, they are treated like VIPs—because they are. Their pristine, delicious produce helps make our menu sing.

The Berkeley market is social. Being a small business owner/restaurateur means I'm often behind the stove or in front of the computer. It can be isolating. It's nice to have times in the week when you get out and talk shop with other chefs or have a chat with a farmer or farm stand manager. We're all part of a larger community. Going to the market reminds me of that. I'm not thinking about staffing issues or plumbing problems. It's about the food and the people who grow it.

Diners often harbor a stereotype about Indian food: that it's static, especially on the vegetable end. It's not all cauliflower, peas, and potatoes at JBC. That's not my style. In the spring I might use tender wilted fava leaves in a side dish. Come summer, we're adding all kinds of juicy heirloom tomatoes to salads. In fall sweet persimmons get plenty of play. And when winter rolls in,

we embrace the earthy goodness of root vegetables and dark leafy greens. Yes, cauliflower, peas, and potatoes are on the menu. But the amazing abundance and variety Northern California farmers produce mean we're able to serve so much more. It's classic Indian cuisine with a modern, Cali twist. That's my jam. Providing a sense of place on the plate—local food cooked in Oakland—is paramount to everything we do at JBC.

━━━━━━━━━━

Sophie Bassin, one of my now sometime servers—she was a steady front-of-the-house employee for the first two years—is also a farmer. She co-runs Feral Heart Farm in Sunol, a slip of a community just 30 minutes from downtown Oakland that feels like it's much farther from urban life. Sunol gets frost in the winter and serious sun in the summer—unlike the fog-engulfed cities by the bay—making it ideal for growing peppers, okra, tomatoes, and other heat-seeking produce.

Feral Heart is a just one of several one-acre farms in the Sunol Water Temple Agriculture Park, managed by the Berkeley nonprofit Sustainable Agriculture Education (SAGE) on San Francisco Public Utilities Commission land.

The AgPark is an affordable option for novice farmers who want to grow close to city markets. It's got funky farm charm: The AgPark boasts a Beaux Arts–style water temple, an unexpected piece of architecture in the middle of ag land, along with a hodgepodge of tiny farm plots.

Sophie started the farm with Aaron Dinwoodie. Both had a bunch of previous farming experience to bring to the project. Working at JBC offered Sophie some financial stability—and a ready-made market—while she worked to get the farm up and running. Now in its third year, Feral Heart Farm benefits from Sophie's food justice background and city contacts. Bubbly, tattooed, and embodying queer community and spirit, in the beginning Sophie worked the fields a few days a week, these days she's tending more to the marketing side of the operation.

We receive two orders a week from Feral Heart. I look forward to seeing what's in those boxes. I'm willing to take produce not in its usual form, color, or shape and get creative with it. The scale of our respective businesses matches up: This is a small farm servicing a small, forty-five-seat restaurant. I can text Aaron or Sophie and ask them to grow specific vegetables or herbs for JBC. They plant fenugreek just for me. They plant loads of produce I love: red burgundy okra, Jimmy Nardello Italian frying peppers, and baby Indian eggplants; these small, variegated purple Toybox eggplants are adorable. I've gotten hard-to-find greens like amaranth, robust beets, and the pointy green cauliflower cousin known as Romanesco. Sophie challenges me by showing up with ingredients I've never worked with before—such as sweet potato greens—so I get to experiment, which is something every cook craves.

We give a shout-out to Feral Heart Farm on the menu. I know Sophie, who lives just a few blocks from the restaurant, enjoys telling customers who are curious about her farming background and pointing out what they're eating that Feral Heart has grown. Some customers really value that connection. It's a no-brainer for me to support new and seasoned farmers alike. Chefs need what these farmers grow. Over time there's a level of trust that develops between a farmer and a chef. I have confidence in how and what they grow, and I'm jazzed about what they bring me. I can adapt to supply issues, take surplus, deal with misshapen or otherwise imperfect produce, which happily finds a home in sauces without sacrificing flavor.

Feral Heart's name embodies the farm's philosophy, which dovetails with my own. This is a heartfelt operation that's a little wild. They're not textbook farmers, growing tidy row crops just so. They're in this little oasis, out in the elements, where the wild pushes up against the domesticated. They're not status quo; they like to play around the edges. What chef wouldn't want to partner with a farmer with that kind of frisky risk-taking attitude? When they push themselves to try growing different crops that feeds my creative fire.

SEASONAL PICKLES

Makes 4 quarts

1 cup pickling cucumbers,
  cut in rounds
1 cup sweet peppers, julienned
1 cup blue lake beans, cut
  into 1-inch pieces
1 cup summer squash,
  cut into half moons
2 cups white wine vinegar
¼ cup shallots, thinly sliced
¼ cup salt
¼ cup sugar
1 tablespoon ginger, minced
1 tablespoon black peppercorns
1 tablespoon coriander seeds
1 teaspoon cloves
1 teaspoon cumin seeds
2 dried chile de árbol

Pickles are essential in the Indian kitchen. We make a variety of different pickles all year round. One of the most common pickling methods we use is a hot vinegar–based brine loaded with aromatics. This recipe utilizes summer vegetables, but it could just as easily include winter vegetables like beets, cauliflower, or Brussels sprouts.

Toss the cucumbers, peppers, beans, and squash together in a medium bowl. Then place the vegetables into a plastic or glass container that can hold all the ingredients with 2 inches of room at the top. Heat the vinegar, shallots, salt, and sugar with 2 cups of water in a medium saucepan on high heat. While the brine heats, combine the whole spices in a dry sauté pan on high heat. When the spices begin to smoke slightly—in about 3 minutes—remove them from the heat and drop them directly into the warm brine. Stir well and let the brine come up to a boil. When the brine starts to boil, reduce the heat to low, and let it simmer for 10 minutes. Then turn the heat off and pour the brine over the vegetables. All ingredients should be fully submerged in the brine. Let this mixture cool at room temperature. Then refrigerate for at least 48 hours. The pickled vegetables will keep refrigerated for up to 2 months.

ASIAN LONG BEAN PICKLE

Makes 1 quart

1 tablespoon neutral oil

1 teaspoon cumin seeds

1 teaspoon nigella seeds

1 tablespoon ginger, minced

1 teaspoon turmeric powder

1 teaspoon Indian red chili powder

4 cups long beans, cut into
  1-inch pieces

¼ cup white wine vinegar

1 tablespoon salt

Every summer we get a bounty of Asian green and purple long beans from Feral Heart Farm. The beans work well in vegetable curries and other hot dishes, but these pickles are my favorite way to eat them. They retain their crunch and have just the right amount of spice and tang for my taste.

Heat the oil in a large sauté pan on high. Add the cumin and nigella seeds. Let the spices sizzle for about 1 minute. Add the ginger, turmeric, and chili powder and stir for about 30 seconds. Add the long beans and stir to coat them with the spices. Let the beans cook for about 2 minutes on high heat. Add the vinegar and simmer for about 1 minute, slightly reducing the liquid. Season with salt and cool. These pickles can be enjoyed immediately but will improve in flavor after a few days in the refrigerator. They can be stored in the fridge for 2 weeks.

STONE FRUIT CHUTNEY

Makes 1 quart

1 tablespoon neutral oil
1 teaspoon cumin seeds
1 teaspoon nigella seeds
1 tablespoon ginger, minced
4 cups diced stone fruit (such as
   peaches, nectarines, and plums)
1 teaspoon turmeric powder
1 teaspoon Indian red chili powder
½ cup granulated sugar
¼ cup white wine vinegar
1 tablespoon salt

We make fruit chutneys all year round, modifying the ingredients depending on the season. I like them all, but summer stone fruit chutney probably tops my list. That said, you can make this chutney with apples, pears, persimmons—even rhubarb—and we do. Keep in mind, you will need to adjust the amount of sugar and vinegar to balance the sweetness and acidity of a particular fruit. For example, tart rhubarb will need more sugar and less vinegar than sweet peaches.

In a large sauté pan heat the oil on high. Add the cumin and nigella seeds and sizzle for 1 minute. Add the ginger and stir to keep the spices from sticking. After the ginger has begun to cook, browning on the edges, add the fruit and stir vigorously to release any pieces stuck to the bottom of the pan. Season the fruit with the turmeric, chili powder, and sugar. Stir continuously to dissolve the sugar. Add the vinegar, season with salt, and lower the heat to simmer. Cook the fruit until it breaks down slightly and the excess liquid reduces. This will take about 10 minutes but can vary depending on the softness or ripeness of the fruit. Less ripe fruit may take longer to soften than overripe fruit. Remove the pan from the heat and let cool. Store the chutney in an airtight container in the fridge for a week.

#HYPERLOCAL

I like sniffing out farm partner opportunities. One of my newest relationships literally popped up across the street from the restaurant. There's this big old corner lot—it's where the neighborhood used to have a seasonal pumpkin patch and Christmas tree lot—otherwise it's basically been this fallow empty space surrounded by a chain-link fence for like twenty years. It's also got a rich history: It's the former site of the X-rated Pussycat Theatre. That's my town. It's about to be developed: Condos are coming. Sign of the times.

So the farm, Top Leaf Farm, is sort of squatting or popping up here before constructions begins. It's all legit—city permits and all. Once the building is up, farmer Benjamin Fahrer is relocating to the roof, so we'll still be able to get his produce. He grows the loveliest mix of salad greens, micro greens, herbs, and flowers. I literally just wandered over there one day, Ben pulled a bunch of produce for me right out of the ground, and that's how we started doing business.

You just never know where or from whom you might find hard-to-source ingredients. My produce distributor, Greenleaf, has championed small,

local farms for four decades. When we first opened, our Greenleaf sales rep Andy Powning, who had been with the company for years, cut branches off his own curry leaf tree in his backyard when they could not find a regular supplier for us.

One of my servers, Teddy, brings me surplus tangelos from his tree; we put the sweet citrus in a delicious preserve for dessert. So many of our customers and neighbors have prolific Meyer lemon trees, which fruit twice a year here and are coveted for their thin, smooth skins, which make excellent zest, and their sweet-tart juice. We pickle and preserve them and use them in vinaigrettes and marinades or add them to dishes as a garnish or sweetly tart accent taste. Come fall, I'm carting Fuji apples and Asian pears from my own backyard trees to the restaurant, where prep cooks chop them into pieces for chutney and chaat.

Oakland may be urban, but there's plenty of backyard bounty around. We're happy to find a good use for neighborhood garden glut at Juhu Beach Club. We find that local growers—many of whom dine with us—are delighted to see the surplus their fruit trees offer on the menu.

SUMMER HEIRLOOM TOMATO SALAD WITH FRESH PANEER

Makes 6 servings

½ cup Preserved Meyer Lemons
  (see recipe page 27)

1 cup neutral oil

3 medium to large heirloom
  tomatoes

1 pint cherry tomatoes

3 sprigs Thai basil

3 sprigs opal basil

6 sprigs cilantro

3 springs mint

2 cups Fresh Paneer (see recipe
  page 197)

3 teaspoons flaky sea salt
  (we use Maldon)

The Bay Area is spoiled when it comes to summer heirloom tomatoes. We have so many varieties in different shapes, sizes, colors, textures, and flavors. We get our heirlooms from several small local farms including Full Belly, Oya, and Feral Heart. This salad pays homage to the traditional, simple Italian Caprese salad, which really lets the tomatoes shine. The preserved lemon vinaigrette adds a tangy and bitter foil to the sweet, juicy, summer fruits.

In a blender, purée the preserved lemons until smooth and creamy. On medium speed, slowly pour in the oil to emulsify the dressing. Wash and cut the heirloom tomatoes into wedges and rounds for visual and textural variety. Wash the cherry tomatoes and cut in half. Pick all of the herbs off their stems and arrange them in a stack on top of each other. Use a sharp knife to chiffonade the herbs or slice them into long thin strips. Toss to mix. Toss the tomatoes with the lemon vinaigrette and then arrange the tomatoes on individual plates. Arrange teaspoon-size chunks of fresh paneer on the plate and sprinkle both the tomatoes and cheese with sea salt. Garnish with the herb chiffonade.

CRISPY FRIED JIMMY NARDELLO ITALIAN PEPPERS

Makes 4 to 6 portions

12 Jimmy Nardello peppers

1 cup white wine vinegar

2 tablespoons Indian red chili powder

2 tablespoons salt

2 cups chickpea flour

1 teaspoon turmeric powder

3 quarts neutral oil

1 cup Cilantro Chutney (see recipe page 46)

When I was a child, my parents hosted dinner parties and served snacks for guests to enjoy at cocktail hour. Most of these tasty bites revolved around deep-fried potatoes, cauliflower, and onions. The one veggie snack I had a hard time eating was the skinny, light green Indian chile. I loved the flavor, but as I got closer to the seeds, it proved too spicy. In the farmers' market I discovered the Jimmy Nardello, a large, mild Italian pepper that offers a similar texture and flavor without the heat jolt. Serve this deep-fried pepper as a party snack with cilantro chutney or with a small green salad as an individual starter.

Wash the peppers and place them on a cutting board. Use a small paring knife to cut a slit in the peppers from the tip all the way to the stem. Leave the stem intact. In a small bowl whisk together the vinegar, chili powder, and salt. Dip the peppers in the seasoned vinegar one by one and then pour the excess vinegar mixture on top of the peppers. Let them marinate for an hour or two. In a medium bowl combine the chickpea flour and turmeric, season with a pinch of salt. Whisk in 1 cup of water and keep mixing to remove any lumps. The batter should be the consistency of pancake batter—thick but pourable. Heat the oil in a medium saucepan to 350°F for deep-frying. Check the temperature with a thermometer. Dip each pepper into the batter to coat it inside and out, and drop them into the oil one by one. Cook until they are crispy and browned on the outside. Serve with cilantro chutney or a salad.

CORN OFF
THE COB

Serves 4 to 6

4 tablespoons unsalted butter
1 lime, juiced
2 teaspoons Indian red
  chili powder
2 teaspoons sea salt
  (we use Maldon)
2 teaspoons neutral oil
1 medium shallot, julienned
6 corn cobs, husked with kernels
  cut off the cob with a sharp knife
1 cup sweet peppers (such as bell
  peppers, padron, shisito), julienned
1 cup green beans (such as blue
  lake, haricot vert, romano),
  cut into ½-inch pieces
Fenugreek Pesto
  (see recipe, page 168)
6 mint leaves, finely chopped

Summer corn from nearby Brentwood—grown with non-GMO seeds—is some of the sweetest corn I've ever tasted. Look for corn at the farmers' market between June and September for peak flavor. All over India, little street stalls sell grilled corn on the cob, as well as corn off the cob served in a small bowl. Both versions are usually seasoned with lime, chili powder, and salt. I grew up eating this kind of corn at every family barbecue. This dish marries my love of both traditional spiced Indian corn with American-style corn slathered with butter and includes other seasonal veggies, though corn is the star.

Let the butter sit out at room temperature for about 30 minutes until it is very soft. Stir the lime juice, chili powder, and salt into the butter and whisk until thoroughly combined. Spread the butter onto a piece of plastic wrap and roll this into a log. Tie the plastic wrap at both ends and chill the log in the refrigerator for at least two hours, so the butter forms a solid cylinder.

Remove the butter from the fridge and cut into ½-inch pieces. Heat the oil in a large sauté pan on high until the oil shimmers. Add the shallot, corn, peppers, and beans and season with salt. Continue to sauté for about 5 to 7 minutes, until the vegetables start to slightly soften. Add the diced butter, stir to melt the butter, and mix with the vegetables thoroughly on medium heat.

Spread a tablespoon of fenugreek pesto on each plate, and evenly distribute the sautéed vegetables on top. Garnish with mint leaves.

FENUGREEK PESTO

Makes 2 cups

¼ cup garlic, minced
¼ cup pistachios, roughly chopped
½ cup white wine vinegar
1 tablespoon salt
1 bunch fresh fenugreek leaves
1 cup neutral oil

One of our farm partners, Feral Heart Farm, grows fenugreek leaves especially for us. In addition to using fenugreek traditionally, such as in our chicken curry, I find other ways to incorporate the earthy, herbaceous leaves on our menu. I recommend tossing grilled vegetables with fenugreek pesto or spreading it on fish before broiling.

In a blender combine the garlic, pistachios, vinegar, and salt, and purée until the mixture is thick and creamy. Add the fenugreek leaves, pushing them down to submerge them as much as possible in the liquid. Run the blender again to purée the leaves into the mixture. With the blender running, slowly pour in the oil in a steady stream. The sauce should thicken and emulsify.

CHILI PANEER

Serves 4 to 6

2 cups neutral oil (for frying)
1 pound paneer cheese
   (store-bought instead of homemade,
   in this case, for texture)
2 tablespoons neutral oil
½ red onion, julienned
2 cups peppers, julienned
   (such as a mix of bell peppers,
   padron, and shisito)
1 cup Cherry Tomato Chutney
   (see recipe page 86)
1 cup Tamarind Pepper Sauce
   (recipe follows, page 171)
1 cup Thai basil, picked leaves
4 cups summer greens, julienned
   (we use arugula, amaranth,
   and mizuna)

Chili Paneer is an Indian-Chinese influenced starter that we typically serve during the summer, since most of the vegetables traditionally used in this recipe are at their peak during that season. Look for U.S.-produced paneer at large grocery stores—especially those with an Asian food aisle—or at Indian grocery shops. Paneer is a fresh cow's milk cheese that is popular in India. I usually see what looks good at the farmers' market and switch out vegetables every few days based on what I find, which adds variety while the heart of the dish remains the same.

Heat the oil in a shallow pan on the stovetop to about 300°F. Check the temperature with a thermometer. Dice the paneer into bite-size pieces, approximately ½-inch cubes. Fry the paneer in the oil until it is lightly browned on all sides, about 2 minutes. Remove the paneer from the oil with a mesh "spider" or slotted spoon. Set it aside on paper towels to drain the excess oil.

In a large wok or heavy-bottom sauté pan heat the other oil. Add the onion and peppers, season with salt, and cook for about 5 minutes until vegetables start to soften. Add the tomato chutney, tamarind pepper sauce, and paneer, and simmer on medium heat until the paneer begins to soften and the sauces reduce—about 5 minutes. Add the basil and greens and stir to combine thoroughly. When the greens wilt—about 2 minutes—portion the paneer and vegetables on individual plates or serve family style.

Tamarind
Pepper Sauce

Makes 1½ cups

1 cup white wine vinegar
2 tablespoons Date Paste
  (see recipe page 25)
1 tablespoon Tamarind Paste
  (see recipe page 23)
3 cloves garlic
1 tablespoon peppercorns

In a medium saucepan combine all the ingredients with 1 cup of water. Heat on high until the liquid comes to a boil. Then lower the heat and simmer for about 10 minutes until the solid ingredients begin to soften. Remove the pan from the heat and allow the mixture to cool slightly, about 15 minutes. Purée all the ingredients in a blender to make a thick sauce.

FALL CHICORY AND DUCK SALAD

Serves 6

2 boneless duck breasts
2 tablespoons Chai Masala
   (see recipe page 111)
½ cup whole almonds, skin on
1 teaspoon neutral oil
salt
3 quarts mixed chicories
   (such as frisée, radicchio,
   Treviso, escarole, puntarelle,
   castelfranco, endive, etc.)
Tamarind Citrus Vinaigrette
   (recipe follows, page 173)
3 ripe pears (such as Bosc or Comice),
   thinly sliced
½ cup dried cranberries

I met Jim Reichardt of Sonoma County Poultry through an industry friend at a winery on the Russian River. I enjoyed our chat over a glass or two of wine and wanted to find a way to work his beautiful products onto our menu. Although he has ducks all year round, the vegetables in season in the fall really speak to the flavor of poultry. This salad combines a number of sweet and bitter ingredients, a balance that mimics the "bittersweetness" of this time of the year.

Preheat the oven to 350°F. Use a sharp knife to score the skin on the duck breasts, cutting only into the skin not the flesh at a diagonal about ¼ inch apart from each other. Place the duck breasts on a tray and rub them with the chai masala to coat evenly. Lay the duck breasts skin-side down in a room temperature sauté pan and place it on medium-low heat. This allows the fat to slowly begin to render; leave the duck breasts on the heat untouched for at least 5 minutes. Look for browning on the edges of the meat. When the skin is browned and crisp, flip the duck breasts over and place them on a baking tray. Put the tray in the oven and cook for 10 minutes. Test for doneness: The duck should be firm to the touch. Remove the tray from the oven and let the meat rest for at least 10 minutes. When you are ready to serve, thinly slice the breasts on a bias.

Toss the almonds with the oil and a pinch of salt. Roast in the oven for about 3 minutes, until the almonds begin to brown. Let them cool and then roughly chop. Set the almonds aside for garnish.

To make the salad:
Julienne the longer greens like the radicchio; tear smaller greens, and remove the root and pull apart the frisée. Soak the greens in cold water and spin in a salad spinner to remove any dirt. Toss the salad in the tamarind vinaigrette with the duck and pears. Plate on individual plates or one big platter. Garnish the salad with the roasted almonds and dried cranberries.

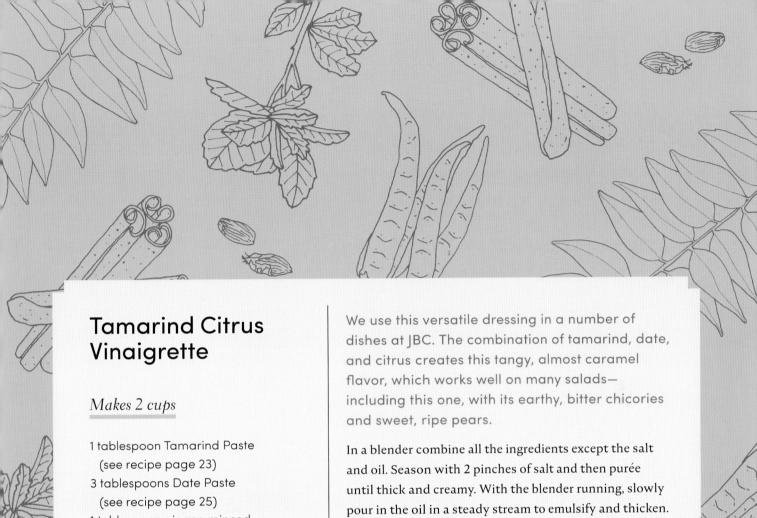

Tamarind Citrus Vinaigrette

Makes 2 cups

1 tablespoon Tamarind Paste
   (see recipe page 23)
3 tablespoons Date Paste
   (see recipe page 25)
1 tablespoon ginger, minced
1 teaspoon Toasted Cumin
   (see recipe page 25)
¼ cup fresh lemon juice
¼ cup fresh lime juice
2 teaspoons salt
1 cup neutral oil

We use this versatile dressing in a number of dishes at JBC. The combination of tamarind, date, and citrus creates this tangy, almost caramel flavor, which works well on many salads—including this one, with its earthy, bitter chicories and sweet, ripe pears.

In a blender combine all the ingredients except the salt and oil. Season with 2 pinches of salt and then purée until thick and creamy. With the blender running, slowly pour in the oil in a steady stream to emulsify and thicken. Season with salt to taste.

BHEL SALAD
(PUFFED RICE SALAD)

Makes 6 servings

6 cups puffed rice (called *mumra*
    in Indian groceries)

2 Peruvian purple potatoes,
    cut into small pieces

2 teaspoons salt

1 pomegranate

½ cup Tamarind Date Chutney
    (see recipe page 53)

½ cup Cilantro Chutney
    (see recipe page 46)

2 diced Fuyu persimmons

1 cup Citrus Pickled Onions
    (see recipe page 26)

1 cup Sea Salt Curried Peanuts
    (see recipe page 176)

½ cup Sev (see recipe page 195)

¼ bunch of cilantro,
    roughly chopped

Bhel is a street food snack found all over India. But it is most often associated with Mumbai. Puffed rice combines with sweet and spicy chutneys, and a handful of usual suspects: like potato, diced onion, and chickpeas. In keeping with tradition, our bhel has puffed rice and chutneys at its core. But from there, the JBC Bhel Salad, served in a Mason jar, departs from custom and includes a mixture of seasonal ingredients. The version here is made in the fall, but you can adapt this dish as the seasons change. In the summer we use cucumbers, cherry tomatoes, and fresh green garbanzo beans. The presentation in the jar keeps the puffed rice from getting soggy until you are ready to eat it. Plus it looks pretty cool.

Preheat the oven to 300°F. Lay the puffed rice on a baking sheet. Place the baking sheet in the oven for about 5 minutes; the rice should be crisp but not brown. Remove the sheet and let the rice cool. Place the diced potatoes in a small saucepan with cold water to cover, add a pinch of salt, and put it on high heat. When the water comes to a boil, test a potato for doneness, using a knife or fork. The potatoes should be just cooked through—about 7 minutes. Drain the potatoes, and spread them out on a baking tray to cool—at least 10 minutes.

Cut the pomegranate through the center, horizontally. Hold the pomegranate over a bowl of cold water and tap it with the back of a spoon to release the seeds. The seeds will sink to the bottom of the bowl and the white pith will float on top. Skim off the pith and drain the pomegranate seeds.

(recipe continues)

To assemble the salad:

Use a medium glass jar, such as a Mason jar. Start with one tablespoon of each chutney in the bottom of each jar. Then layer in a small scoop of the persimmon, potato, pomegranate, and pickled onions. Top it off with the curried peanuts, equally distributing them in each jar. Fill jar from here almost to the top with puffed rice, and garnish with sev and cilantro. Serve jar inside a bowl. When ready to eat, empty all the ingredients from the jar into the bowl and mix together.

Sea Salt Curried Peanuts

2 cups raw peanuts
2 tablespoons neutral oil
1 tablespoon Curry Powder
  (see recipe page 110)
1 tablespoon salt

These peanuts are easy to make and versatile: enjoy as a snack or a topping on ice cream.

Preheat the oven to 350°F. Toss all the ingredients in a bowl. Spread the mixture on a sheet pan and bake it in the oven for about 10 minutes, until the nuts are golden brown. Let it cool for at least 15 minutes. The nuts will keep in an airtight container at room temperature for up to 1 week.

BRUSSELS SPROUTS
WITH CURRY LEAF GINGER BUTTER

Makes 6 servings

3 pounds Brussels sprouts

1 medium garnet yam

1 medium sweet potato

1 medium purple potato

¼ cup neutral oil

2 tablespoons Chaat Masala
(see recipe page 106)

3 tablespoons Ginger Curry Leaf Butter
(recipe follows, page 177)

2 tablespoons salt

½ cup Fenugreek Pesto (see recipe
page 168)

3 sprigs fresh mint

This dish is a popular vegetable side or starter in the fall and winter at JBC. It's a big hit at Thanksgiving gatherings. The addition of the sweet potato adds just the right amount of natural sweetness to temper the bitter, salty sprouts. And the curry leaf ginger butter brings a delicious richness to the dish.

Trim the ends off the Brussels sprouts and quarter them. Peel all three potatoes and cut them into a 1-inch dice. Place the potatoes in a medium saucepan with cold water and a pinch of salt and bring to a boil. Cook for 7 minutes. Drain the potatoes in a colander and let them cool. In a large sauté pan, heat the oil on high, until it is just about smoking, and then add the Brussels sprouts. Coat the vegetables and continue to cook them for about 10 minutes—stirring every so often—until they are cooked. Add the potatoes and stir to combine. Season with the chaat masala, ginger curry leaf butter, and salt. Stir to fully mix all elements. The butter will melt and begin to brown the edges of the vegetables. Spread 1 tablespoon of Fenugreek Pesto on each plate, top with the sautéed vegetables, and garnish with the mint.

Ginger Curry Leaf Butter

Makes 2 cups

2 cups unsalted butter

2 teaspoons ginger, minced

20 fresh curry leaves

In a small saucepan heat the butter, ginger, and curry leaves on medium heat. When the butter is fully dissolved, lower the heat and cover the saucepan to infuse the flavors. This butter can be used in either liquid form or cooled in the refrigerator for at least two hours, so it forms a solid that can be cut and added to a sauté pan. Keeps in the refrigerator for two weeks.

A DAY IN THE LIFE OF JUHU BEACH CLUB, FEBRUARY 7, 2017

Tuesday is the restaurant's Monday, as the latter is a traditional dark day in the restaurant industry. Monday, in fact, is the only day JBC is closed. Here's a snapshot of a typical Tuesday, from morning prep to dinner service and beyond.

—Sarah Henry

9:30 AM

It is a wet winter morning. Preeti is at Navi Kitchen—her about-to-open casual counter-service spinoff in nearby Emeryville. Coming soon: Indian pizza with chaat masala frying peppers, burnt masala-brined rotisserie chicken, and tikka masala mac. Today, though, her first order of business doesn't revolve around food, she's getting quotes for grease trap servicing and dealing with smashed glass, courtesy of a homeless person, caught on security camera.

The glamour of restaurant life.

Meanwhile, Melissa, the chef de cuisine for both Juhu Beach Club and Navi Kitchen who has worked for Preeti for two years, is the first to arrive at JBC.

Melissa does a quick survey of what's in the refrigerator and what needs prepping. She comes up with a to-do list. It seems daunting: Holy Cow Short Rib Curry, Uncle's Chicken, Pork Da-Beli, Sloppy Lil' P, Vegetable Curry, Braised Chicken Leg, Sticky Wings, Chili, Sweet & Sour Sauce, Ghee, Ghost Pepper Chutney, Desi Jacks. Spice blends: Chai, JBC Garam Masala, Kids' Chicken.

Her priority at the start of the week: marinating and braising meats.

The petite, dreadlocked African American single mom from East Oakland, a seasoned restaurant cook, is the consummate multitasker. The scent of roasting peanuts permeates the air. She's prepping vegetables: peeling potatoes, chopping onions, and cutting cauliflower for the Sloppy Lil' P. She's also salting and searing short ribs, making a chicken marinade. Melissa is efficient, strong, unhurried, focused, and fast—really fast.

Munira, whom Preeti half-kiddingly refers to as her mini-me, holds down the fort at table 40, the de facto staff table. She works her laptop and phone, organizing vendor accounts for Navi, slated to open in the spring. She checks in with restaurant supply stores for new equipment. Munira, an Indian American working on a PhD at UC Berkeley, worked the line at JBC in Oakland on and off for about two years during her studies, before heading up the since-shuttered Hong Kong JBC outpost for nine months. Another proficient multitasker, she fields reports from recipe testers for this book. Deadlines loom on many fronts; she takes it all in stride.

Meanwhile, Armando mans a tiny station in the back by the dish sink, peeling and processing a pile of ginger. Then he moves on to serrano chiles.

Glance in there every once in a while and you find him bouncing to the salsa playing on his phone. The lanky Mexican American has a winning smile.

Armando and Melissa have a warm, easy camaraderie; they help each other out. They like to laugh—cackle really. They're also dialed in on the jobs at hand.

10:00 AM

Preeti is in the house. She checks reservations for the evening, eyeballs boxes of pavs, the Greenleaf produce drop. Then she dons an apron, cranks some tunes: Frank Ocean Pandora channel. She asks Melissa what she can do to help her work her way through that to-do list. They joke about the role reversal.

For the first two to three years of JBC, most of this prep was handled by Preeti—mostly solo.

Melissa asks her to start on Desi Jacks, Ghee, Kids' Butter Chicken Sauce, Ghost Pepper Chutney. Preeti grabs a bright blue glove to handle the ghost peppers, which she'll roast with garlic. She pulls beets from the oven that have been simultaneously roasted and steamed. She separates liquids from solids for the ghee. And she starts a masala spice tray. It's all seemingly happening at once, amid chatter and check-ins about what's in-house food-wise and what's cooking with the kitchen crew.

There's a steady calm to all this activity. Lots of tempting smells waft in the air. I'm hungry. Preeti senses peckishness in the house, mine and others.

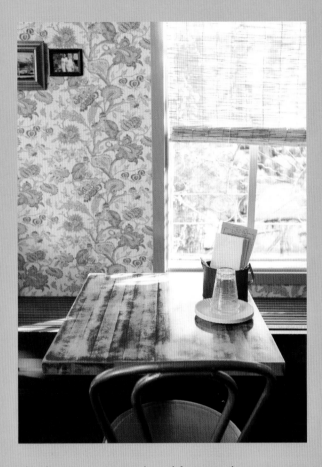

She fixes everyone a breakfast snack: leftover chai-spiced bacon and melted cheese on toasted, day-old pavs. We scarf those sliders down.

Sheila, the neighborhood panhandler has set up shop outside the Check Cashing business across from the restaurant. Sheila is a serial hugger; Preeti and Melissa have a soft spot for the woman, who can be combative, depending on her mood.

The delivery guy from Preferred Meats, Carlos, drops off boxes at the delivery door. Melissa checks the order and chats with Carlos. Preeti points out that the culture at JBC is inclusive: everyone matters, everyone plays a role in getting food on the table. The

The smell of roasting garlic fills the restaurant. Popcorn pops. Four burners simmer with sauces and curries in various stages of doneness.

Melissa returns with a big bag of onions. There's good-natured banter: which sales rep most brightens her day? Hands down the young Indian American man pushing paper and plastics. Danish stops by to check on supplies, and sometimes he'll hang out at table 40, checking his email and chatting with Preeti, who ribs him for not having eaten at the restaurant while still feeling free to suggest new menu items. She's nicknamed him Gajar, which means carrot in Hindi, after the sweet carrot dessert he thinks JBC should make. Everyone's a critic.

Melissa grabs a giant wooden paddle and starts mixing the elements for the braised chicken, including onions, butter, and tomatoes, in a large pot on the stove.

Butter and salt and onions are a constant in the kitchen throughout the day.

vendors and delivery drivers are part of the extended JBC family. Monterey Fish Market drops off shrimp; there's a coffee delivery from High Wire.

11 AM

Photographer Alanna Hale arrives. She's here to capture process shots for this cookbook. Her energy is playful, yet unobtrusive. She's on a mission, too.

Melissa realizes the kitchen is low on onions. So she makes an emergency onion run to Temescal Produce, conveniently located across from the restaurant. The owner, Jamal, who hails from Yemen, is friendly and accommodating. He's bailed the cooks out on more than one occasion.

NOON

Melissa powers through her list, taste-testing and adjusting seasoning as she goes. She enjoys the food at JBC and sits down to family meal with her cooks when her schedule permits, but with two young sons, she mostly eats dinner at home. Besides, the menu prices, she says, are a bit steep for someone on her wage.

Preeti is in good spirits. It's been a while since she's worked Tuesday prep.

Chef is in her kitchen groove; it's a respite from being tethered to a laptop dealing with the business side of running one restaurant and opening another. On a sheet pan rack in the open kitchen one pan sports white tape. Written on the tape in black Sharpie: "Preeti's shit. Do not touch." Her favorite knives and kitchen tools live here.

The conversation moves between preferred mop heads, what Preeti might pick up at the farmers' market, and how many especially hot rogue peppers courtesy of Oaktown Spice Shop she should add to the ghost pepper chutney. She drops one in. Melissa eggs Preeti on. Add another. They giggle. Done.

Armando whistles to music only he can hear. Later, he'll come out of the dish room and sing in English, whatever is playing in the restaurant. He knows some lyrics, the women tell me, even if he doesn't understand the meaning of the words. The universal language of love songs—it's adorable.

The vibe is familiar, cheery, cozy, relaxed, respectful. Getting set up for service is front and center.

There are much worse ways to spend a workday, and everyone in here knows it.

1 PMish to 3 PMish

Munira jumps into Preeti's car to do errands. First stop: Egg noodles from a particular store in Oakland's Chinatown.

Preeti and Alanna run out between rain showers to take pictures with a grower who is bringing rooftop farming to apartments scheduled for construction across the street. Preeti's a fan of Farmer Ben's greens, herbs, and radishes. The pair swing by the Berkeley farmers' market to take produce and vendor pics and to Ben's rooftop farm in Berkeley, in a new apartment complex housing university students.

Melissa keeps methodically working her way down the list, crossing off items once they're completed. She changes the music channel: She's a reggae gal.

City parking enforcement swings by, visible to the open kitchen. There's a mad dash to move cars. Melissa and Armando dodge tickets. But Munira is too late to prevent Preeti's beacon of a bright mango Mini from getting a sixty-dollar fine. It's a cost of doing business. Sigh.

When Preeti returns from errands, she's greeted by an unexpected visit from besties Gretchen and Geeta and their two kids, three-year-old Naveen and newborn Leela. They happened to be in the neighborhood for playgroup and ate tacos afterwards next door. Naveen acts like the restaurant is his second home. And it sort of is. Gretchen helped out with carpentry work at JBC before it opened. The family comes in for special events— like birthdays—and casual dinners, too. Everyone happily and quickly catches up—this is chosen family—and then back to the tasks at hand.

3:30 PM

Line cooks Alek, Kaitlin, and Marisol arrive. Kaitlin, a tall ginger, immediately sets up the pantry station. She checks the status of sauces, chutneys, pickles. Where she sees a need or a surplus of certain produce, she'll make a new batch. She stores greens in large containers for the fridge. Her energy is languid, dreamy. But she gets stuff done, too.

The diminutive, dark-haired Alek scoffs down a tangerine, asks Melissa what needs doing, and jumps in to make the vegetable curry. She grabs a sticky, food-stained orange binder and double-checks the recipe's ingredients. Then she goes about her business in an independent, I've-got-this manner.

Marisol, another petite cook (milk crates come in handy for this crew), has already worked a full day stocking Silicon Valley kitchens. Five days a week she leaves her San Jose home around 3:30 am, drives to her Palo Alto job, then nine hours later she heads to her second shift at JBC. It's at least an hour's drive, depending on traffic, which can be hideous. She wants to save money in the expensive Bay Area. Although this schedule seems unsustainable, the long day and stressful drive don't show: Marisol is a flurry of activity at the fry station. She makes the batter for the Manchurian Cauliflower. She blanches the fries. She uses an ice-cream scoop to shape the potato patties for the Vada Pav. Then she looks for other jobs that need doing and starts wrapping and storing pavs.

There's not a lot of idle talk. This kitchen trio have their heads down, working.

Melissa picks up her pace, she wants to get everything done before her shift ends.

4:30 PM

Front of house staff, Drew and Ayele, arrive. Drew rocks a black ensemble and pairs it with bright pink lips. She begins wiping tables and arranging flowers—purple and red anemones that Preeti's brought back from the market.

Ayele is relatively new to Juhu. Her resume includes stints at several notable area restaurants. She sets up the bar. On a typical Tuesday, two servers work the floor. Ayele, whose face is framed with a shock of curls, is reserved at first. But she makes a point of stressing how refreshing it is to work in a restaurant that values, respects, and supports staff who are women, people of color, queer, or all three. It's rare, she says, and a big deal.

5:15 PM

Preeti changes the music to Andre 3000. The house lights are dimmed.

Preeti's on the line tonight—she's making sure her systems are in place. When she sees holes, she expects her staff to plug them. She reminds Kaitlin to add pistachios to the Winter Citrus Salad. She walks Alek through how to cut the beef short rib for maximum impact. The two discuss plating the dish. She nudges Marisol to set up her station in time for service, which starts in 15 minutes.

While Brussels sprouts sauté and fingerling potatoes cook, Preeti does a quick check-in with servers about a change on the menu—Holy Cow Short Rib Curry replaces the Lamb Kofta. They ask questions about saucing, spicing,

ingredients so they're up to speed. There's a quick discussion about any reservations of note.

Melissa clocks out, her to-do list complete. She's off to pick up her boys.

5:30 PM
Doors open.

A sign above the entrance reads: "Welcome all: shapes, sizes, colors, sexes, languages, cultures, beliefs, ages, preferences, statuses, faiths. You are home."

A sticker in the window signals the restaurant's sanctuary status: "Sanctuary Restaurant. A place at the table for everyone."

A woman walks in moments later. Ayele greets her. The customer says: "Just a table for one." Ayele responds warmly: "Perfect, this way please." Service has begun.

A couple of other solo diners follow; folks fresh off work in for dinner and a drink at the bar.

6:00 PM
A consistent flow of couples walks through the doors, headed to two-tops. Also in the house: drivers picking up orders for DoorDash, Postmates, and other food delivery services. That's when Drew and Ayele discover that the payment system, Breadcrumb, is down. It's not the first time.

There's a flurry of activity around the iPad designated for payments, in an attempt to fix the problem. No such luck. Preeti calls HQ and discovers it's a system-wide glitch. Plan B: Digging out the manual credit card swipe machine from the attic. A half hour later, the service comes back online.

6:30PMish to 8:30PMish

The restaurant is full. But no one is waiting for a table. In other words, a standard Tuesday night in February. I ask Alanna, who lives in San Francisco, to describe the crowd: Diverse, she says, in terms of age and ethnic background. True that: carefully dressed hipster Oakland queer couples, next to older Berkeley hippies in, ah, eclectic attire, next to casually clad mixed race families. Colleagues, friends, solo diners. A hodgepodge of people. No one demographic dominates.

VIPs in the house tonight include a group from New York, who work with Ann, Preeti's wife and JBC co-owner. Around 8 o'clock Ann stops by to greet the group. They've already started on their cocktails, which come with a bowl of Desi Jacks, compliments of the house. They're comfortably settled into a back booth.

There's a growing conversational buzz in the room punctured by hearty laughter.

A couple Ayele knows comes in. She's surprised and delighted to see them. Next, a group of friends who asks a member of their party: "What should we order?" Her response: "I don't know. I was only here once on a first date." Clearly, it wasn't the food that was foremost on her mind that night. Drew walks them to a booth and through the menu.

A steady stream of salads, pavs, curries, and cauliflower exits the kitchen. Preeti moves smoothly between back and front of house. She brings dishes to tables and checks in with guests, who enjoy the attention from the chef/owner.

There's an older Indian man out with a friend, to whom Preeti delivers a Bhel Salad, served in a jar. She explains that the contents, which she describes, are tipped into the accompanying bowl and mixed. It meets with interest, approval, and dinner table small talk.

Alanna and I eat at the bar. A man comes in for pickup. We chat. His toddler daughter, who just had brain surgery, is in stable condition at nearby Oakland Children's Hospital. I pop a menu in his takeout bag, figuring he'll be back.

A woman at the bar asks for menu recommendations. No worries. Her friend joins her for dinner, and they move to a table. Preeti insists that everyone in her extended family is well fed, so before Alanna leaves she is loaded up with food to take to her partner, Arlo, now at home in the city.

Alanna is on her way out as Brian, of Starter Bakery, walks in. He makes Preeti's pavs. Brian pops by for a quick dinner. It's been a while. The two business owners are close; they speak the same language, a kind of small food biz shorthand, and enjoy a laugh. Brian and Preeti catch up on each other's news over a drink. They commiserate about plumbing problems, discuss staffing concerns, share industry gossip.

8:30 PM

A quick check-in of the line reveals a mix of food being cooked and plated for service and raw ingredients getting processed for the next day. In the back, Armando is buried in dishes. As they

have for the past three hours, guests come and go, come and go.

9 PM

The tables have noticeably thinned out; a few "closers" linger. Front and back of house cleanup commences. Ayele folds napkins and flatware for the next day. Drew wipes tables.

Line cooks put food away in labeled and dated plastic tubs, take stock of their stations, clean and clear.

Preeti grabs a bottle of wine as she heads out the door with Ann, whose work colleagues have already left the building. Preeti fields a text from Melissa: She has been in a car accident—hit by another vehicle. Her car is totaled. She's shaken and has a sore knee, but otherwise is okay. Thankfully, her boys weren't in the vehicle.

9:30 PM

The last diners have left, and the front door is locked. The kitchen crew continue to pack, wipe, clear, clean, sweep. Drew tallies the till and fills the safe. Ayele does a final front of house spot check. Armando washes the last stack of cookware. Garbage and compost go out. During close, crew members might sip a beer or glass of wine as they do these end-of-service tasks; a quick staff dinner might feature surplus prepared food from the line or an impromptu pasta using extra produce and proteins from the fridge.

Then it's swift goodbyes as staff head to their cars or bikes or the bus.

Tomorrow, many of the same crew will be back to do it all over again.

Chapter Six

SIGNATURE
DISHES

I never aspired to do fine dining. I had a taste of working in that environment, briefly, right out of culinary school. It's not me or my aesthetic. I like creating food that is lusty, a little messy (but intentionally so). I don't like over-manipulated ingredients. I want them to shine on their own merits with just a little assistance from the kitchen. I have spent years (even when cooking California cuisine in other people's restaurants) training cooks how to plate dishes that are visually appealing but don't feel forced. New cooks often want to put elements of a dish in straight lines or make towers with component ingredients. That approach could not be farther from my plating philosophy. We color outside the (straight) lines at JBC. I like my plated dishes to look natural, organic, without a lot of fuss or froufrou flourishes, but still with an attention to aesthetics.

When we first opened JBC, I thought it was going to be a pretty casual place. Over the four years we've been running the restaurant it's morphed into so much more than a pav shop. In the first year or so I quickly discovered that our regular customers appreciate having a chef-driven Indian restaurant with a seasonal, evolving menu.

JBC devotees seem especially excited when new dishes pop up on the menu, along with their favorites. These diners embrace our take on Indian food, reimagined through a California lens, and they want more. After the first nine months of operation we closed the restaurant for two weeks over the winter holidays. Ann and I went to Mumbai. It was our first trip to India without my parents. It was both daunting and exciting. We went, in part, in search of new ideas for JBC. It was a much-needed vacation. It was also a serious restaurant research trip.

We had a pretty demanding eating agenda. Some days found us sampling from hole-in-the-wall momo shops we stumbled upon in our explorations. We tucked into the delicate-yet-juicy pork-and-vegetable-filled dumplings. On another day, we committed to a three-hour lunch over a nine-course tasting menu at Masala Library, a temple to modernist Indian cuisine. The restaurant, run by renowned chef Jiggs Kalra, incorporates molecular gastronomy techniques with Indian classics in mind-blowingly imaginative ways. The unassuming spot, housed in a bland office complex and devoid of flashy decor, is all about the food. My favorite dish: a contemporary take on that ubiquitous Indian snack known as *jalebi*, the syrupy, sticky swirls of deep-fried dough that melt in your mouth. The Masala Library version reinvents the dessert as tiny beads of "caviar" dough made to resemble salmon roe, floating in a pistachio broth and topped with saffron foam. It was a beautifully deconstructed dish and every bite burst on the tongue with a surprising surge of sweetness.

From the humble to the refined, I found inspiration in it all. The casual Swati Snacks, a modern vegetarian diner, is so good that people wait forty-five to ninety minutes for a seat at their sleek, elegant tables. And they don't even serve booze. Swati Snacks offers a lot of my favorites: dosa, idli, pani puri, *dhokla* (a steamed, savory lentil cake), and *khandvi* (a pasta-like roll made from chickpea flour and yogurt). The *panki chatni* there is a standout. Panki chatni is a superthin savory rice-flour crêpe steamed in a banana leaf and served with spicy mint chutney and green peppers. Finger-licking goodness. I'm still trying to figure out how to introduce that dish in my own restaurant.

Ann and I navigated the city as a couple, but there were no romantic PDAs. The irony, of course, is that many people of the same sex—men or women—routinely walk down the street in India holding hands or with arms linked. It's a cultural thing. We visited my cousins, and even though on a recent visit my family had explained the nature of our relationship, Ann was still asked where she lives. We've lived together for twenty years.

Such disclosures in India make many people uncomfortable and nervous. Gayness is a taboo topic in so-called polite company. Gay sex is also illegal. I joked with Ann that that fact just makes intimate moments in India that much more titillating because they're illicit.

On our way home we stopped in London for a few days to get a flavor for how Indian food has evolved in the country of my birth. Ann and I were particularly wowed by the design, pop culture influences, and branding aspects of Indian-influenced restaurants in the city—such a fashion-forward town. We sampled modern food at fun, casual, irreverent places with a hip aesthetic—these travel experiences served to reinforce what I thought to be true: that a new generation of Indian restaurants is popping up all over the world.

Obviously London has deep roots when it comes to Indian cuisine, and it was cool to see the creative license and reimagining of the genre in a city with an international reputation—for better or worse—for corner curry shops.

The trip was rejuvenating in other ways. Ann and I had run ourselves ragged launching the restaurant. I'd worked twelve- to fourteen-hour days, five to six days a week, for close to a year. Meanwhile, Ann worked her day job and spent her "free time" helping with all the myriad details needed to keep a restaurant operating: picking up menus at the printer, going to the bank, buying extra glassware. There is always something to be done, something that demands attention—now. We hardly saw each other for twelve months, and when we did, I was always exhausted. It was an incredibly challenging year in our relationship, and we desperately needed time alone, just the two of us, to reconnect as a couple and to reflect upon our shared vision for the restaurant. There's a reason a lot of personal relationships don't survive the demands of running a restaurant: It's hard on family life.

When we returned, in January 2014, I was refreshed, pumped up, bursting with ideas about how to take the JBC menu to new places: zucchini fritters, okra fries, steamed clams in a green garlic saffron broth. At first it was scary. There's always a risk as a chef when you introduce new dishes: There's a learning curve training cooks on different recipes and skills. And there's a risk with diners, too. We'd won customers over with our street food, would they come along for the ride and try new menu items?

With the exception of the clams—which might have been too big a leap at the time for diners not used to Indian-influenced restaurants serving sustainable seafood—our guests have responded with enthusiasm. And I never give up: That steamed clam dish will come back on the menu one of these days; it's delicious. It's about building trust with your guests. I think we're good on that score.

The Manchurian Cauliflower, a sweet-and-sour concoction that's now a signature dish on the menu, can be traced to that trip to Mumbai. Ann was so enamored with the versions of this Indo-Chinese dish she tried there she insisted I make it. We taste-tested a ton, from casual restaurants, takeaway joints, street food stands. Some were too goopy or not crispy enough, but the good ones were undeniably good.

Ann had a hunch my take on the classic, deep-fried, sweet-and-sour-sauce smothered dish would be a hit. And my lovely wife is rarely wrong. Piled on a plate, it's a glossy temptress that oozes drama and excitement. The uninitiated can't wait to try it; the seasoned eater can't get enough. It is hands down our most popular dish today. We slice the cauliflower two ways, giving eaters different textures to chew on. We add carrot and onions to ours to enhance the taste and texture of the dish and coat the vegetables in a fenugreek mustard masala. Our version is super crispy—and, no surprise here—heartily spiced.

I seesaw between traditional approaches and modern riffs. Indian restaurants usually serve boneless chunks of meat in a pool of creamy sauce flecked with vegetables that rarely venture away from the standard potato, cauliflower, and spinach. My curries feature chunks of in-season fresh vegetables and meat cooked on the bone, like a whole chicken leg or lamb shank. I use fenugreek in ways that are "typically" Indian—as in curries—but I also employ the slightly sweet, nutty-flavored herb to make pesto and salsa verde.

Similarly, our signature Sev Puri is a hybrid of traditional technique and modern ingredients. Our crispy house-made puri, a deep-fried circular bread, is topped with garnet yam smash, Pink Lady apple chunks, pickled red onion strips, turmeric-seasoned sev pieces (chickpea-flour noodles we make from scratch), and finished with a drizzle of two chutneys. It's a pretty ensemble on an individual plate. There's no pretty way to eat it, though, but that's not the point. It proves an excellent gateway dish. Puris are synonymous in my mind to getting a party started. Crunchy, fun, playful, messy: marrying tradition with the unconventional.

As much as I buck tradition in my cooking, I am also a stickler for doing things the "right way." For me that means making food from scratch, with respect for traditional techniques. I may serve a sev puri that is three times the size of a typical one, topped with non-traditional ingredients like nectarines, but we make our puris by hand every day. We make the sev in-house, too. That's a value that I hold dearly: food crafted by hand, not a factory.

No one in the JBC kitchen now or when we opened had ever cooked Indian cuisine professionally before they came to work for me. I trained all my cooks—a couple of them have been of Indian background, but most of them not—and they execute my vision on a daily basis with skill and integrity. In the current industry climate—where restaurant owners from fast casual to fine dining bemoan a shortage of sous chefs and line cooks—attracting and retaining talented kitchen staff is tricky. My small cooking crew makes me proud. Sure, I need people who know how to use a knife and can handle the heat when the house is full and the orders keep coming. But when I'm hiring, I tend to put more emphasis on attitude than experience. I can teach cooks how to prep spice blends, put up pickles, braise meats, make ghee, cook rice (yes, that's a learned skill), and assemble everything into a coherent dish. I can't correct a bad attitude, but I can fix a sauce that's missing something or made with the wrong yogurt. It happens.

That approach comes with its own challenges: Sometimes it takes a while before the staff's skill set is up to the task of tackling a new dish in prime time. Dishes like the lamb biryani, which is a multiday process with our housemade, rough puff pastry, would not have been possible the first year we opened. Now it's routinely on the menu—who doesn't like a potpie?—and I'm not the only one who can make it. To continue to thrive, a restaurant needs to constantly raise the bar, try new things. That's the kind of culture I strive for at JBC.

In many ways, four years into the restaurant, I feel like I've only just cracked the surface of what we can do. Food is an evolving thing. You can't be static or stagnant with your menu. I've got a larger, long-term vision. Stay tuned.

SEV PURI

12 puris (recipe follows, page 194)

3 cups sev (recipe follows, page 195)

2 cups fresh green garbanzo beans (can substitute fava beans)

½ cup whole plain yogurt (we use Straus)

1 tablespoon Toasted Cumin (see recipe page 25)

6 nectarines, pitted

½ cup Citrus Pickled Onions (see recipe page 26)

¾ cup Tamarind Date Chutney (see recipe page 53)

Cilantro Chutney (see recipe page 46)

1 cup cilantro, finely chopped

Sev puri is a very common and beloved street food dish all over India. Bite-size crispy puris—a kind of deep-fried dough—are topped with a variety of seasoned vegetables like potato, chickpeas, and onions. The puri is then drenched in chutneys, yogurt, and crispy sev—a crunchy noodle. We make our puris and sev fresh in-house daily. To make sev from scratch requires an inexpensive special tool (called a sancho), available at Indian grocery stores or online. Alternatively, packaged sev and puris can be purchased at an Indian grocer or online. We change the ingredients in this dish seasonally. The recipe here is made in summer, when fresh green garbanzo beans make an appearance at farmers' markets.

First prepare the puris and sev according to the recipes.

Heat a medium saucepan filled with water on high and season with a pinch of salt. Remove the garbanzo beans from their pods. Fill a medium metal bowl with ice water. When the saucepan water comes to a boil, drop the beans into the boiling water for about 2 minutes. The beans will begin to float to the top of the water. Use a slotted spoon to remove the beans from the pot and drop them directly into the ice water. Drain the beans when they are fully cooled—about 10 minutes.

In a food processor purée the beans, yogurt, cumin, and a pinch of salt. The purée should be thick and spreadable but not watery. Set the purée aside. Dice the nectarines into small ½-inch cubes. Finely chop the onions and mix them with the diced nectarines.

To assemble the puris:
Spread each puri with a thick layer of the garbanzo bean spread. Top this with a tablespoon each of the tamarind chutney. Divide the nectarine mixture evenly between the puris. Drizzle each puri with the cilantro chutney and garnish with crispy sev and cilantro.

Crispy Puris

Makes 18 to 24 puris

2 cups all-purpose flour
    (+½ cup for dusting)
1 teaspoon salt
1 teaspoon black pepper,
    freshly ground
2 tablespoons Ghee
    (see recipe page 22)
¾ cup warm water
3 quarts neutral oil (for deep-
    frying)

A wide variety of different breads in Indian cooking fall under the umbrella term of *puris*. Puris are generally small to medium size and deep-fried. Depending on the different flours, grains, and seasonings used—along with cooking time and technique—puris can be crispy or soft. We use a small, skinny Indian rolling pin called a *belan*—widely available at Indian or Asian grocers. It's worth the minimal investment to roll out perfectly round puris.

In a mixing bowl combine the flour with the salt and pepper. Make a well in the center and pour in the ghee and warm water. Using a stand mixer fitted with a dough hook, mix the dough on medium speed for about 5 minutes. Turn off the mixer and check the dough's consistency. The dough should be smooth but not sticky. If the dough is not smooth, add a few drops of water and continue mixing for another minute or two. If the dough is sticky, add a tablespoon of flour and mix again. When the dough is smooth and forms a ball, remove it from the mixer and wrap it in plastic wrap and let it rest for at least 30 minutes. The dough can be chilled in plastic wrap for up to 3 days in the refrigerator.

Heat the frying oil in a medium saucepan to 350°F. Use a thermometer to check the temperature. Use a dough cutter to cut off a quarter of the dough at a time. Keep the dough under a moist towel to prevent it from drying out. Roll the quarter by hand into a log, about a ½-inch thick. Then cut off 1-inch long pieces; they will look a little like gnocchi. Press the two cut ends of the dough to form a small thick round.

Roll each portioned dough piece into a thin round about 5 inches in diameter. Use a small paring knife to make ½-inch-long slits all over the dough, this will keep it from puffing up in the frying process. Drop the puris into the hot oil one at a time. Flip each one over after the first minute to ensure even frying on both sides. Remove each puri after about 3 to 5 minutes, when it is crispy and golden brown on both sides.

Sev

Makes 2 quarts

1 cup chickpea flour
1 teaspoon turmeric powder
1 teaspoon salt
⅓ cup warm water
3 quarts neutral oil (for deep-
  frying)

Sev is a crispy chickpea noodle served in bite-size pieces. It's a common garnish for Indian street food, adding a salty, crunchy dimension. An inexpensive metal hand tool called a sancho is needed to make the noodle. This noodle maker can be found at Indian grocery stores or online. Sev keeps in an airtight container for up to 2 weeks.

In a medium bowl combine the chickpea flour, turmeric, and salt. Make a well in the center and add the warm water. Use a small rubber spatula and stir to fully combine. The consistency should be thick—like playdough. Heat the oil for frying to 375°F. Use a thermometer to check the temperature. Fill the sancho with the chickpea batter and squeeze the skinny noodles that extrude into the hot oil. Sev will only take a couple of minutes to get crispy. Remove the sev and cool on paper towels to drain any excess oil.

PEACHES AND PANEER

Makes 6 servings

6 sprigs fresh mint

12 sprigs fresh cilantro

3 scallions

3 slices white bread
  (we use Pullman loaves)

½ cup Ghee (see recipe page 22)

3 cups Fresh Paneer
  (recipe follows, page 197)

1½ cup Stone Fruit Chutney
  (see recipe page 161)

Creamy fresh cheese pairs well with sweet and spicy condiments. My take on this combination matches sweet stone fruit with handmade Indian cheese. The paneer is a cow's milk cheese that is simple to make. It requires a fine cheesecloth, available at kitchen supply stores or online. Substitute fresh ricotta or goat cheese for home-made paneer if preferred, but don't use prepackaged paneer from a supermarket as an alternative in this instance; it's too much of a solid block for this dish.

Pick the mint leaves and cilantro leaves off their stems and toss them together in a small bowl. Cut the scallions very thinly on the bias. Rinse the scallions in cold water a few times to remove any excess sliminess. Toss the scallions with herbs and set them aside. Cut the crusts off the bread and cut the bread into 6 triangles. Brush the bread triangles with the ghee and lightly toast them on both sides for about 3 minutes. Use an ice-cream scoop to divide the fresh paneer into 6 balls. Place the paneer balls on a baking sheet lined with parchment paper.

To assemble the dish:
Preheat the oven to 350°F. Place the sheet of paneer in the oven to warm for about 5 minutes. To serve, the paneer should be gooey but not falling apart. Heat the toasts in the oven on a separate baking sheet for about 3 minutes. Place the toast on each plate and place a warm paneer ball on top. Cover each ball with the fruit chutney. Season the herbs with salt. Serve the peaches and paneer on individual plates with a handful of herb salad.

Fresh Paneer

Makes 1 quart

½ gallon whole milk
2 teaspoons fresh lemon juice

In a heavy-bottom, medium saucepan heat the milk on medium high, stirring to keep the temperature even in the pot. As the milk warms, it will start to rise in the pot. When the milk comes to a boil, add the lemon juice and stir. The milk solids will start to curdle and separate from the liquid or whey. Spread two layers of cheesecloth over a sieve or colander. Pour the curdled milk over the cheesecloth, and allow the whey to seep out.

Tie off the cheesecloth and refrigerate it with a weight on top of the colander to release any excess liquid. Chill the paneer for at least 3 hours. When ready to use, the paneer should be somewhere between fresh ricotta and cream cheese in consistency. The paneer will keep in an airtight container for about 3 days.

EDIBLE EXCURSIONS, EDIBLE EDUCATION

Sarah Henry met Preeti Mistry when they both served as tour guides for Edible Excursions. Preeti's guide gig was short-lived, she led tours of San Francisco's Ferry Building and Mission District in the year prior to opening JBC.

Sarah went on to curate the company's Oakland expeditions. As luck and timing would have it, the Temescal tour, a three-hour eating jaunt through the neighborhood, launched the week Juhu Beach Club opened in the spring of 2013.

These days, Sunday public tours begin at Juhu, which guests frequently refer to as Juju. No matter: it's the food and the restaurant chef that stick in folks' memories.

Sarah shares tales from these field trips here.

"This food is not suitable for the American palate. Not suitable." One of my tour guests is trying to convey that she can't handle the heat at JBC. Fair enough, everyone's palate is different. Nonetheless, her delivery rubs me the wrong way.

I'm not sure how to respond. The cranky reporter in me wants to say: "What's the American palate, and who gets to decide what's suitable or not?" The underlying assumption here seems to be it's not appropriate for a white person's tastes.

But I'm wearing my hospitality hat today, polling guests at the end of an Edible Excursions tour on their favorite places along the way. Typically, JBC is at the top of the list of six stops. Guests are frequently delighted by the restaurant's playful vibe, unexpected food, and charming, chatty chef. I simply say: "Thank you for your feedback—I'll let chef know."

And I do. Preeti shrugs off the concern; she's heard similar sentiments before. JBC accommodates both heat seekers and those whose taste buds tend to the milder side, hence the lightning bolts on the menu, indicating dishes that are particularly fiery.

As a concession to the heat-adverse, guests usually get a heads-up from me prior to the tour now: JBC is our spiciest stop, exceeding the fire factor of both the Korean and Ethiopian restaurants in the mix. Most guests welcome the chance to sample food from a restaurant that isn't interested in dumbing down dishes for an Anglo-centric audience. Juhu is unapologetically hot. Deal with it.

In the beginning, when the restaurant wasn't open on Sundays, Preeti used to come in and cook just for our guests. These early patrons were delighted to get a sneak peek into JBC, the buzzed-about newcomer hidden from plain sight. Guests, mostly an assortment of Bay Area locals curious about Oakland's hella cool restaurants, are typically an adventurous bunch hungry for new edible experiences.

Preeti is a hit with the food tour set. She doesn't assume knowledge or patronize; she's just really enthusiastic about what she does and why, and guests respond to her passion for food craft and culture. She has this impish quality and youthful, lively energy that guests respond to, even while she doesn't shy away from tough topics. There's a reason she made the cut for *Top Chef*—and guests who watch reality TV food shows recognize her from Season 6—or, more recently, from an episode of Anthony Bourdain's *Parts Unknown* that paid homage to Oakland in general and JBC in particular.

These days, JBC is open for business on Sundays. We start the tour here now, so guests are in and out before the brunch crush builds. Servers introduce the food; I fill in for Preeti with an abridged version of the JBC story if she's spending a rare morning at home. Guests taste signature menu items including a Vada Pav, the potato puff slider that packs serious heat courtesy of the ghost pepper chutney. Cooling iced chai, a Sassy Lassi (mango and yogurt), or a Nimbu Pani, cumin-spiked lemonade with a cilantro haze float, complement the food.

Preeti packs each guest a little container of Desi Jacks for the road. In typical Chef Mistry style she wants to give guests a reminder of the restaurant to take home.

MANCHURIAN CAULIFLOWER

Serves 4 to 6

1 medium cauliflower
1 large carrot
1 yellow onion
1 tablespoon Mustard Fenugreek
  Masala (see recipe page 102)
1 tablespoon black salt
2 tablespoons Indian red chili powder
1 teaspoon kosher salt

For the sweet and sour sauce:
1 cup tomato paste
1 cup granulated sugar
1 cup white wine vinegar
2 tablespoons ginger, minced
2 teaspoons Indian red chili powder

For the batter:
3 cups all-purpose flour
2 cups cornstarch
4 quarts rice oil (for deep-frying)

For the garnish:
¼ cup cilantro, roughly chopped

This is by far the most popular dish at the restaurant: If we took it off the menu there might be a customer revolt. Manchurian Cauliflower is an Indian-Chinese classic. Our take on the dish—which marinates for a few hours—has a few more add-ons than the classic version, but it is still very much rooted in tradition.

Remove the outer green leaves and stems from the cauliflower, and cut the head down the middle in an X to make four wedges. Lay the wedges cut-side down and make thin cross-sectional slices of each piece. After cutting a cauliflower wedge about halfway, turn the piece and chop the rest of the wedge into bite-size florets. This cutting technique provides different textures of cauliflower. Peel the carrot and cut it on the bias into thin slices about 2 inches long. Halve and peel the onion. Cut half moon slices of onion. Mix all the vegetables together and season with the mustard fenugreek masala, black salt, chili powder, and kosher salt. Set the vegetables aside for 2 to 4 hours.

To make the sweet and sour sauce:
Combine the tomato paste, sugar, vinegar, ginger, and chili powder in a medium saucepan on medium-high heat. Bring to a boil, lower the heat, and simmer for about 15 minutes, stirring occasionally. Remove from the heat.

To make the batter:
Combine the flour and cornstarch in a large bowl. Pour 5 cups of water into the bowl a cup at a time and mix with a large whisk until a thick runny pancake batter consistency is reached.

(recipe continues)

For the first fry:

Heat the oil for deep-frying to 300°F in a heavy-bottom pot. Check the temperature with a thermometer. Dip the cauliflower mix into the batter in batches and drop into the hot oil. Use a mesh "spider" or slotted spoon to move the cauliflower mixture around to keep it from forming large clumps. When the mixture begins to lightly brown—about 3 minutes—remove and place the cauliflower on paper towels to drain any excess oil. Continue cooking the cauliflower mixture in batches. Compost any excess batter.

To finish and assemble the dish:

Increase the heat in the fryer to 375°F. Check the temperature with a thermometer. Drop the fried cauliflower mix back into the hot oil for about 5 minutes, until golden brown and crispy. Remove the cauliflower from the oil. In batches, toss the cauliflower mix in a metal bowl with the sweet and sour sauce. Garnish with the cilantro.

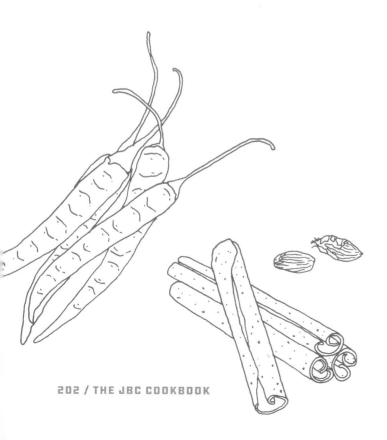

CHICKEN WINGS TWO WAYS:
VINDALOO & STICKY VERSIONS

Makes 6 servings

4 pounds chicken wings

2 quarts Vindaloo Marinade
  (see recipe, page 42)

4 quarts neutral oil
  (for deep-frying)

½ cup cilantro, roughly chopped

Vindaloo Sauce and Blue Cheese
  Raita or Sticky Sauce (recipes follow,
  see page 205)

These two different kinds of chicken wings have the same beginnings in our vindaloo marinade. Both are finger-licking delicious and best if marinated overnight. The Vindaloo Wings are closer to a traditional buffalo wing, relying on lots of butter and a blue cheese dip or raita for its flavor. Sticky Wings offer a sweet sauce to balance the tanginess of the marinade.

Cut the wings into individual joints if they are still connected. Make small slits in the chicken flesh to let the marinade absorb into the meat faster. Cover the wings with the vindaloo marinade and refrigerate for at least 12 hours, ideally overnight.

When ready to cook, remove the wings from the marinade and use your hands to scrape off any excess solids clinging to the chicken.

Heat the oil in a heavy-bottom pot on high to 300°F. Use a thermometer to check the temperature. Fry the wings in batches until they are cooked—about 5 minutes at a time. Remove them from the fryer and drain any excess oil on a paper towel. Increase the heat to 375°F. Check the temperature with a thermometer. Fry the wings a second time on the higher heat until they are browned and crisp on the outside. Toss them with your sauce of choice in a large metal bowl. Garnish them with cilantro and serve with the blue cheese raita for the vindaloo version or with toasted spices for the sticky sauce version.

Vindaloo Sauce

Makes 3 quarts

2 quarts Vindaloo Marinade
(see recipe page 42)
½ pound unsalted butter
1 cup tomato paste
2 tablespoons salt

Heat the marinade in a medium saucepan. Whisk in the butter and tomato paste. Continue to whisk to keep the butter from separating. Season with salt. When the sauce comes to a boil, reduce the heat to low and simmer for about 10 minutes. The sauce may separate. If it does, use either a small immersion blender or countertop blender, and pulse to recombine the ingredients.

Blue Cheese Raita

Makes 1 cup

¼ cup soft, crumbly blue cheese
(we use Point Reyes
Farmstead Original Blue)
½ cup whole plain yogurt
(we use Straus)
1 teaspoon Toasted Cumin
(see recipe page 25)

In a food processor, combine the blue cheese, yogurt, and cumin. Purée until smooth and transfer to a bowl for dipping.

Sticky Wings Sauce

Makes 3 quarts

2 quarts Vindaloo Marinade
(see recipe page 42)
2 cups granulated sugar
1 cup tomato paste
1 tablespoon cumin seeds
1 tablespoon nigella seeds

Heat the marinade in a medium saucepan. Whisk in the sugar and tomato paste. Keep whisking to dissolve them into the marinade. When the sauce comes to a boil, reduce the heat to low and simmer for about 10 minutes. Season with salt.

Toast the cumin and nigella seeds in a dry sauté pan on high for about 3 minutes. Transfer the seeds to a bowl to cool. After the seeds are cool, grind them to a fine powder in a spice grinder.

MASALA FRIES

Serves 6

6 russet potatoes

4 quarts of neutral oil (for deep-frying)

¼ cup Chaat Masala
  (see recipe page 106)

2 tablespoons salt

Tamarind Ketchup (recipe follows,
  page 207)

Ghost Pepper Yogurt
  (recipe follows, page 207)

Cilantro Chutney
  (see recipe page 46)

Making fries from scratch at home might seem daunting, but it's actually pretty easy. These simple, spicy fries are a staple at Juhu. They work well on their own as a snack or as a side accompanying a pav or the Bombay sandwich. We serve these deep-fried treats with three different dipping sauces. Now, that's a party.

Scrub the potatoes to remove any excess dirt. Use a mandoline or sharp knife to cut the potatoes into long strips. Rinse the potatoes in cold water. If you are not cooking them immediately, cover the strips with cold water to prevent browning.

Heat the oil in a heavy-bottom pot to 300°F. Use a thermometer to check the temperature. Fry the potatoes in batches for about 5 minutes. The potatoes should be cooked through on the inside but not browned. Remove the potatoes from the oil and cool. Increase the oil heat to 375°F; use a thermometer to confirm the temperature. In batches, fry the potatoes again until crisp and brown —about 2 minutes. Toss them in a bowl with the chaat masala and salt. Serve with tamarind ketchup, ghost pepper yogurt, and cilantro chutney for dipping.

Tamarind Ketchup

Makes 2 cups

½ tablespoon Tamarind Paste
  (see recipe page 23)
3 garlic cloves
1 lemon, juiced
1 teaspoon Indian red chili
  powder
2 cups ketchup

This ketchup is based on a sauce my family refers to as "public sauce." Public sauce doesn't have any particular recipe, but is simply about starting with a dollop of ketchup and then adding whatever is in the fridge to enhance the flavor. At home, we'd add this spicy sauce on the side for dipping deep-fried muhogo (cassava fries), or crispy pakoras (a vegetable snack).

In a blender combine all the ingredients, except the ketchup, with ¼ cup of water. Blend until puréed. Fold this mixture thoroughly into the ketchup. Serve.

Ghost Pepper Yogurt

Makes 2 cups

½ cup Ghost Pepper Chutney
  (see recipe page 53)
1½ cups Greek yogurt
½ tablespoon salt

I like to think of this dipping sauce as the JBC aioli. It's definitely a bit healthier than standard mayo or aioli. The Greek yogurt gives the sauce a luscious, thick, creamy feel and balances the kick from the ghost pepper.

Combine all the ingredients, taste, and add more salt if needed.

BACON FRIED RICE
AKA THE HANGOVER CURE

Makes 4 servings

8 slices bacon, roughly chopped

½ cup fresh curry leaves

1 tablespoon brown mustard seeds

1 cup red onion, julienned

1 cup red bell pepper, julienned

1 cup green beans, cut into 1 inch pieces

2 cups lacinato kale, julienned
  (also known as dinosaur
  or Tuscan kale)

1 cup diced mango

4 cups cooked Turmeric Lemon Rice
  (see recipe page 226)

2 teaspoons Indian red chili powder

4 eggs (we use cage-free eggs)

2 teaspoons neutral oil

4 tablespoons Ghost Pepper Chutney
  (see recipe page 53)

I can't guarantee that this fried rice will cure your hangover, but it will help ease the pain. It's also a good way to use up leftover rice: My mother would often make fried rice on Saturday or Sunday for lunch. She never wanted rice to go to waste. Her version included curry leaves, mustard seeds, and a decent hit of heat. My vegetarian mother's version didn't have bacon or eggs. But for adult me, bacon and eggs equals breakfast or brunch. The addition of fresh mango helps balance all the salty and spicy elements. Feel free to swap out the peppers, beans, and kale for other seasonal vegetables that you might have on hand such as mushrooms, Brussels sprouts, and chard in the fall or winter.

Place the chopped bacon in a small saucepan with a ¼ cup of water on high heat until the water begins to boil. Reduce the temperature to low and let the bacon slowly render, about 20 to 25 minutes. When the bacon is almost fully browned, remove from the pan and strain the excess bacon fat on paper towels. Separately, set aside both the bacon and the leftover fat from the pan.

Heat a large sauté pan or wok on high for 1 minute. Add 4 tablespoons of the bacon fat, the curry leaves, and the mustard seeds. The ingredients will sizzle and pop at first and then start to subside. After about 1 minute, add the onions, peppers, and beans. Stir frequently to soften. Once the vegetables begin to soften, add the kale, mango, and bacon. Continue to stir. After 3 minutes add the rice and chili powder and stir to incorporate all the vegetables with the rice. Continue to cook on medium heat. Some of the rice may stick to the bottom of the pan.

To cook the eggs, heat the oil on medium in a nonstick skillet. First crack the eggs in individual bowls to make sure the yolks stay intact. (Eggs with broken yolks can be used for scrambles or omelets.) Slip each egg into the pan and fry them until the whites are fully cooked—about 5 minutes— when the white is fully set.

To assemble the dish:
Taste the rice for seasoning and adjust the salt as needed. Arrange the rice and vegetables in 4 bowls. Top each bowl of rice with some ghost pepper chutney and a fried egg.

HOLY COW SHORT RIB CURRY

Makes 6 servings

6 beef short ribs, bone in

3 tablespoons salt

¼ cup neutral oil

1 yellow onion, julienned

2 tablespoons ginger, minced

2 tablespoons serrano chiles, minced

¼ cup Smoky Black Cardamom Masala (see recipe page 104)

6 cups whole canned tomatoes

1 pound fingerling potatoes

1 pound parsnips

1 pound jumbo carrots

1 tablespoon salt

This recipe started out as a pav filling at JBC, but it proved so popular—and we fielded so many requests for the meat on its own—that the dish morphed into a main meal. The name is a play on my Hindu upbringing and our belief that the cow is a sacred animal. Neither of my parents ever eat beef, but they never limited their daughters from trying meat. These days, I'm happily—holy cow—carnivorous. The spice blend in this dish is a perfect match with slow-cooked beef.

Preheat the oven to 350°F. On the stovetop heat a heavy-bottom pot or casserole on high. Season the short ribs with salt on all sides. Add the oil to the pan and wait until it is very hot and starts to smoke. Sear the short ribs in the oil and brown on all sides, in batches if necessary, depending on your pan size. Once the meat is well browned on all sides, remove the ribs from the pan and set aside.

Lower the heat to medium and add the onion. Stir with a spoon, scraping to release the browning in the pan. After about 3 minutes—when the onions have begun to soften and become translucent—add the ginger and chiles. After 5 minutes more, add the masala and stir for another 2 minutes to mix thoroughly. Add the tomatoes, using a spoon to scrape any remaining bits that have stuck to the bottom of the pan. Break up the tomatoes with the spoon. Season with salt to taste.

Return the short ribs to the pan with the sauce; make sure they are almost fully submerged in the liquid. Cut a piece of parchment paper big enough to cover the top of the pan and press it onto the surface of the ribs in the sauce. Cover the pan tightly with aluminum foil and place it in the oven. Braise the ribs for 3 hours, then check them for doneness. The meat should easily fall away from the bone. If the meat does not pull away easily, return it to the oven for another half hour and check again. When the ribs are fully cooked, remove them from the heat, and remove the ribs from the braising liquid. Skim the top of the braising liquid to remove the excess fat with a cold, wet spoon. When the sauce is skimmed of all excess fat, return the ribs to the sauce.

While the ribs are cooking, blanch the vegetables. First wash the fingerling potatoes and place them in a pan of cold water with a pinch of salt. Bring the water to a boil and then simmer until the potatoes are just cooked—about 5 to 7 minutes. Peel the parsnips and carrots, and cut them into bite-size pieces, about the same size as the potatoes. Place the carrots and parsnips in a saucepan, and fill it with water and a pinch of salt. Bring the water to a boil and test the vegetables after 3 to 5 minutes—they should be easily pierced with a small knife. Remove the vegetables from the heat and drain.

To assemble the dish:
Add the vegetables to the sauce and ribs. Serve family style with lemon turmeric rice on the side or individually plated with a rib on each plate.

JBC LAMB BIRYANI
WITH ROUGH PUFF PASTRY TOP

Serves 6 to 8

4 pounds boneless lamb leg
  or shoulder, trimmed of excess fat

1 tablespoon kosher salt

1 cup Smoky Black Cardamom Masala
  (see recipe page 104)

2 tablespoons neutral oil

1 yellow onion, julienned

2 tablespoons ginger, minced

2 tablespoons serrano chiles, minced

3 cups whole canned tomatoes

2 cups basmati rice

1 teaspoon saffron

3 tablespoons Ghee
  (see recipe page 22)

1 tablespoon brown mustard seeds

10 fresh curry leaves

1 yellow onion, julienned

8 fingerling potatoes, boiled
  until tender, then halved

6 small carrots, peeled, trimmed and
  boiled until tender

½ pound thin asparagus spears,
  trimmed and cut into 1-inch pieces

For the pastry:

1 pound Rough Puff Pastry
  (recipe follows, page 215)

1 egg

1 tablespoon heavy whipping cream

1 tablespoon cumin seeds

1 tablespoon nigella seeds

The first time I saw a biryani sealed with puff pastry I thought it was a magical move. Marrying a classic Indian rice dish with a French-style pastry struck me as inspired. When I returned to London for culinary school, a puff pastry topped biryani was a popular menu item at several of the palaces devoted to haute Indian cuisine in London at the time. Since I love both biryani and potpies, I decided I had to try my hand at making my own for the restaurant. This dish demands a commitment of time: Ideally the meat should marinate overnight and, once cooked, sit overnight in the refrigerator. It's a good kitchen project for a weekend and well worth the effort, I promise. So set aside some time to make a dish that will impress your dinner guests.

Cut the lamb into 1-inch pieces and season with the salt and 3 tablespoons of the masala. Cover and refrigerate for at least 3 hours or overnight.

Preheat the oven to 350°F. In a large, ovenproof sauté pan or Dutch oven heat the oil over high heat. When the oil is hot, add the lamb in batches in a single layer, taking care not to crowd the pan. Sear the meat, turning the cubes as needed, until it is browned on all sides. Transfer the meat to a bowl and repeat with remaining lamb. When all of the lamb has been seared, add the onions to the pot, season with a pinch of salt, and cook. Stir until the onions are softened and translucent—about 5 minutes. Add the ginger and chiles and cook for 3 minutes. Add the remaining spice blend and cook, stirring, for 1 to 2 minutes, until the spices begin to stick to the bottom of the pan.

Pour in the tomatoes and their juices and scrape the bottom of the pan with a spoon to release any browned bits. Taste and season with salt as needed. Return the lamb to the pot, cover, and braise in the oven until the lamb is soft and fork tender—about 2 hours. Remove the lamb from the oven, let the meat cool completely, and then transfer to the refrigerator and chill, ideally overnight.

(recipe continues)

After chilling, use a spoon to remove any hardened fat from the surface of the braise, and shred the meat by hand or with two forks.

To make the rice:
Place the rice in a strainer and rinse with cold water. Transfer to a bowl, add the saffron and warm water to cover by ½ inch. Soak the rice for 20 minutes.

Heat the ghee on high heat in a medium pot. Add the mustard seeds and curry leaves and fry until the curry leaves are crisp and the mustard seeds start popping—about 2 minutes. Add the onions, reduce the heat to medium, and cook, stirring, until translucent— for about 6 minutes. Pour in the rice and soaking water. The rice should be covered with water by about ½ inch; add more warm water if needed. Bring to a boil over high heat. When the water level reaches the top of the rice and steam channels begin to appear on the surface, reduce the temperature to low, cover, and cook for 15 to 20 minutes. When the rice is cooked, fluff it with a fork.

To assemble the biryani:
Preheat the oven to 350°F. Spoon the shredded meat and sauce into a large Dutch oven. Scatter the vegetables over the meat. Spoon the rice over the top, covering the meat and vegetables entirely.

Remove the puff pastry from the refrigerator and roll out to a thin, even piece large enough to cover the top of the Dutch oven. Lay the puff pastry on top of the rice dish, and seal it by pressing the pastry against the pot edges.

Crack the egg and whisk it with the cream. Brush this egg wash on top of the puff pastry, then sprinkle it with the whole spices.

Transfer the dish to the oven and bake until the pastry is browned and crisp on top, the meat is heated through, and the asparagus is tender, about 20 minutes. To test for readiness: insert a small knife in the center for 10 seconds and check the temperature. The knife should be hot all the way through. Remove the potpie from the oven and let it cool slightly before serving.

Rough Puff Pastry

Yield: 1 pound of dough

215 grams plain flour
   (plus 1 cup for dusting)
4 grams salt
8 grams granulated sugar
162 grams unsalted butter, cold
110 grams water, cold

This is not a traditional puff pastry recipe. It is a simplified version that we use at the restaurant. The recipe ingredients are listed in metric measurements: Pastry requires precise amounts. This recipe makes more than is necessary for the biryani. Freeze any extra pastry for up to three months. If skipping this step, there are decent frozen puff pastry alternatives in supermarkets. My preferred product is the DuFour brand.

Combine the flour, salt, and sugar in a large bowl. Dice the butter into $\frac{1}{2}$-inch pieces, and incorporate it into the flour by hand. Break up large chunks of the butter with fingers. When the butter pieces are about the size of a quarter, add the water and knead the mixture by hand into a shaggy dough. Dust a baking tray with flour. Shape the dough into a rectangle about 2 inches thick. Place the dough on the tray, cover it with plastic wrap, and refrigerate for at least 30 minutes.

Remove the dough from the fridge and roll it into a long rectangle, 3 times the length of the original piece. Fold the top edge down to the middle of the dough. Then fold the bottom on top. Turn the dough so that the seams are on the right-hand side and roll it out again to 3 times its size. Fold the top and bottom in again, wrap the dough with plastic wrap and chill it again for at least 30 minutes.

Remove the dough from the refrigerator, and repeat rolling and folding it twice. Wrap it and refrigerate it again for at least 30 minutes. Remove it from the fridge and roll and fold the dough one last time. The dough is now ready to use. Roll it out to its intended size and thickness and bake.

Chapter Seven

AUTHENTIC?
HELL YEAH!

'm in New York. It's Saturday night, October 15, 2016. I'm on a panel discussion hosted by *Wall Street Journal+* held in conjunction with the Food Network's Food and Wine Festival. The topic: South Asian Food Is Finding Its "It" Moment. I know, I know—cue eye rolling now. But there's interest in a new wave of Indian restaurants popping up around the country that are going way beyond the chicken tikka masala and *saag paneer* shops of yesteryear—curry houses as they're known—that were the dominant motif of first generation Indian immigrants.

Don't misunderstand me—like most people of Indian origin, and many Westerners, too, I have a soft spot for these places. But there is more to Indian cuisine than what's on the menu at many of these restaurants.

And today there's an increasing shift toward what is sometimes referred to as progressive, new Indian cuisine. Some, like me, have roots in the street food camp, while others align with fine dining. Whether upscale or down home, these places often reflect the experience of the second generation immigrant—like me. (Well, technically I'm first generation Indian American, but I've never lived in India.) Just please don't call it Indian fusion. That's a term I loathe. What does that even mean?

The moderator, Pervaiz Shallwani, then a reporter for the *Wall Street Journal* and now a food critic at Newsday, invited me. I think I was supposed to represent the crazy young Californians. We're in this screening room in some fancy Midtown Manhattan private club. It's packed with people.

On the panel: Madhur Jaffrey, the acclaimed Indian actress and global ambassador for the nation's cuisine with a gazillion cookbooks to her name. I'm not going to lie: I'm a big fan of this diminutive octogenarian who turned tons of Anglo-Americans and Brits on to Indian home cookery. Also on the panel: Meherwan Irani, the former car salesman and two-time James Beard Award nominee. He helms the Southern-based, Indian-style street food Chai Pani Restaurant Group, with locations in Atlanta and Decatur, Georgia, and Ashville, North Carolina. He's awesome. Also in the house: Manish Mehrota, the lauded chef behind the high-end, boundary-breaker Indian Accent in New Delhi. A New York location opened in February 2016. Rather than showcase regional cuisine, Indian Accent goes global: dosa with hoisin duck, blue cheese naan, pastrami *kulcha* (a leavened bread)—that kind of thing.

Madhur chimes in first: she's tired of "new" restaurants trying to appeal to American palates and reminisces about honest home cooking by Indian mothers and grandmothers that may be lost in translation to a new generation of Indian food lovers.

I can't help myself. I have to call bullshit on that being the only prism from which to view Indian cuisine. I show respect to both my elder, a legend in the culinary and cinematic fields, and to traditional Indian cooking, which Madhur is so thoroughly steeped in. But the question "what is real Indian food?" feels dated. We need to move on. The second and third generation Indian American experience is just as valid. Our ingredients, techniques, and presentation may not count as so-called traditional, but the heart and soul of our food are Indian.

I'm sort of shit scared to blow my wad this way. But Madhur is gracious and a lively discussion ensues. I argue, as I have for some time now, that the way I cook Indian food is, indeed, authentic.

People's concept of authenticity is some fetishistic idea of what is supposed to be authentic, and it negates the experience of subsequent generations of Indian immigrants. We are authentic, too. When critics ask me if my food is authentic, I say: "Hell yeah, my food is authentic. It's 100 percent authentically me." And when people ask me what region of India my food comes from I tell them: "Oakland."

⁣⁣⁣⁣⁣⁣⁣⁣⁣

Most Americans who only know Indian food from restaurants in the United States, know one particular kind of Indian cuisine, the Punjabi or northern cuisine, known for naan and curry, tandoori, dal, and stews that are brownish or reddish or orangish. But there are so many different styles and regional dishes that hail from the subcontinent.

There's something like 400 types of bread from India. Why get stuck on naan?

Try puffy *bhatura*, often accompanied by the spiced chickpea curry known as *chole*; or the fermented rice-and-lentil crêpe known as dosa, frequently stuffed with potatoes and served with coconut chutney and the lentil dish sambar; or the thin, folded, elastic-doughed roti, typically served with saucy meat dishes.

I wanted to explore my Indian roots through my cooking and make it my own. So many people expect Indian fare to be either a mom-and-pop curry shop or fancy fine dining with white table-cloths and waiters with paisley vests. I'm neither of those things. The only thing paisley about JBC is the wallpaper.

At Juhu, I'm trying to do something nontraditional with nuance. It's influenced by modern Mumbai street eats, California farm-to-table fare, and American comfort food. The notion of whether or not it's "authentic" is incongruous to me.

As a culture, we tend to only ask these questions of certain cuisines—unfairly, I might add. Nobody expects European cuisines, such as French or Italian, to stay in a narrowly defined box. A French chef, for example, may incorporate Japanese ingredients or techniques, but their food is still considered authentic and might be labeled "evolving" or "modern," rather than "fusion." That's not always the case for Indian, Vietnamese, or Mexican chefs who innovate and express different influences. Often such efforts are slapped with the "fusion" label or are somehow no longer seen as "authentic" by critics and customers alike.

I want to take Indian ingredients and techniques and use them in an

intentional way that's rooted in a particular time, place, and culture: Oakland, California, circa 2013 and beyond.

||||||||||||||||||||

Weekend brunch service at JBC has a party-like atmosphere. Motown is the preferred soundtrack to late Saturday and Sunday mornings. Staff bop along while they work. On the line a cook is coating turmeric-marinated chicken through a mixture of corn-starch, yogurt, and a combination of chickpea and rice flours, prepping the poultry for cooking in order to create that crispy coating beloved by fried chicken fans. In the dish room, a new line cook is staging, which is just a jargony way of saying she's trying out in the kitchen. We put her to work on a marinade for the week ahead. There's a mix-up on the yogurt—she uses Greek instead of plain—so we walk her through how to thin the sauce. It's a rookie mistake, no problem.

Meanwhile, Jhe, manning the pantry station, spices the yogurt that accompanies Chumpchi's Channa. He's a gentle giant with a mellow disposition and typically sports a knitted beanie. Next to him, Melissa, his "sister," is ladling doswaffle batter into a Belgian waffle making machine. Jhe is Melissa's cousin, but was raised with her family like a brother.

JBC brunch incorporates traditional Indian flavors and forms with modern tastes and techniques. Take the doswaffle. It's my own invention: the marriage of a lentil-batter South Indian dosa made in the style of a light and fluffy Belgian waffle. We serve it with fried chicken and sweet-and-spicy syrup and black pepper butter. Our classic comes with masala potatoes, sambar, and coconut chutney. And in a nod to the kids in the crowd—or the kids at heart—we offer a Nutella Banana Doswaffle that features the popular

hazelnut spread, brown sugar bananas, and cardamom whipped cream.

Also on the menu: Chai-Spiced Bacon, The Hangover Cure (bacon fried rice, sunny-side up egg, seasonal vegetables, mango, and hot sauce), and a Bombay Sandwich featuring cheese, beets, chaat masala, and cilantro chutney.

Brunch at JBC is a boozy affair. Setting up the bar together are veteran servers Sissy and Teddy, who happen to be good at their job and good friends. Sissy exudes a New Age-by-way-of Burning Man aura. She's also spent several long stints traveling in India. Sissy might wear long feather earrings, a black cap covered in gold skulls, and gold sneakers. She's clear on her job: People who brunch, she says, are coming in for a good time, good food, and a good vibe. Teddy, who favors button-downed shirts, slacks, and ruffled hair, makes the spicy mix for the Bloody Meera, which features scorpion pepper; salt and chile powder line the glass rim. Sissy preps an assortment of add-ons for the drink: celery stalks, cilantro stems, and pickled peppers on a toothpick. That vodka-fueled cocktail is a party in a glass. Teddy polishes champagne flutes for the Mango Mimosa, which features Prosecco and mango pulp. They're ready for business.

Doors open at eleven. Typically, there's a bunch of people waiting to nab a seat. On this sunny Sunday, first through the door are a gay couple sporting bedhead and fashion-forward jeans and shirts in intentionally clashing colors. Good morning! A gaggle of girlfriends—celebrating a birthday—dressed to the nines in heels, toting gorgeous flower bouquets and beautifully wrapped gift boxes, spill through the entrance. They make themselves at home in a back booth and stay through the entire service, a fun bunch. Sleep-deprived parents with wee ones in tow make their way in; upon exiting they leave a trail of fried rice on the floor in their wake. Other diners: A UC Berkeley student and his visiting parents, an Indian American family of four from the outer East Bay, newcomers to the neighborhood, families with teens who aren't particularly interested in being with their parents, though they happily tuck into waffles, fried chicken, and eggs. A group of cute, gay men park themselves at an outside table and soak up the sun. It's a typical JBC motley crew.

Do any of them question the authenticity of the menu? Hell no.

||||||||||||||||||||||

I'm a rebel at heart. I like to stir shit up. And I have no problem speaking out when I see sexism, racism, xenophobia, homophobia, or any other kind of discrimination in this industry. It's my duty. That's part of being authentic, too.

Take the prevailing attitude, for instance, that women are the best home cooks but men can handle the restaurant industry. Or men belong on the hot stations, and women in pantry and pastry. Please. I'm a female running my own shop: I show all my cooks by example that women can handle the heat and deal with the stress of running a small business and be a gracious host. End of story.

And I'm not alone. Thankfully, Oakland is bursting with badass women chefs cooking all kinds of cuisine. The only thing holding us back: women still have a tough time financing new restaurants; finding investors willing to take a chance on a new or expanding restaurateur. That's not typically the case for men. Don't get me started.

Regardless of sexual orientation and ethnicity, nobody in a kitchen should be treated disrespectfully. I think who I am—a queer brown woman of color who can't "pass" as anything else—is one reason I didn't last in traditional restaurants. The militaristic, hierarchical fine dining environment doesn't support someone like me. People who took a chance on me didn't care what I looked like. I knew when I opened my own restaurant I wanted to create a safe space for people like me who feel like other, an outsider, different. There's a home for them here.

||||||||||||||||||||||||

Many adventurous eaters on the hunt for authentic global flavors expect to find cheap so-called ethnic food in urban environments like Oakland. In my mind, such assumptions border on racism. It's certainly classist. Typically, it means eating ingredients of unknown origin, cooked and served by underpaid people, many of them immigrants and/ or people of color. Why should "ethnic" food be cheap? That's another food term—with its underlying assumptions and prejudice—I'd like to see put to bed. Cheap eats, cheap labor: there's a hidden human and environmental cost to that kind of consumption.

I'm not trying to be self-righteous here: we've all eaten inexpensive pho, ramen, dumplings, tacos, *banh mi*, or pad thai at a family-run immigrant restaurant. But we need to recognize that there's a larger cost to these experiences.

Quality ingredients cost more: grass-fed beef, free-range chicken, sustainable seafood, and organic produce are more expensive than factory-farmed meat and conventionally grown crops. It also costs more to make everything from scratch—whether pavs, puri, or pickles.

The term "ethnic food" as a code for "cheap eats" is so engrained in American culture it's hard to escape. It's outdated, and it annoys me. When food critics first started writing about Juhu Beach Club, they called it an Indian restaurant. But I honestly hadn't thought about it that way. I was just cooking what I like to eat: my food.

We get pushback on the price of menu items at times. That's also annoying because I'm not sure that chefs who make their own pasta at an Italian restaurant or prepare coq au vin at a French restaurant experience the same kind of questioning. People just reflexively think that an Indian curry should be cheap. There's no consideration to the steps involved in making everything from scratch, the provenance of the ingredients, the labor-intensiveness of the process—marinating and braising meats. Any one dish might have five or six different components to it.

There's this respect and reverence for the talent and technique that goes into so-called fine dining—which, let's face it, is often white, male, European-influenced. Why shouldn't food cooked by black and brown people be taken seriously and considered worthy? I'm a chef with a diverse background: a person of Indian heritage, who trained and worked in London, who calls Northern California home. My menu, what I'm trying to articulate on the plate, is an expression of all my experiences.

Ever the contrarian, I'm trying to educate people that non-European cuisine can also be elevated and innovative. Thankfully, our diners for the most part get what we're trying to do. We are a value-driven restaurant, and the portions are generous. Nobody leaves Juhu Beach Club hungry.

In the Bay Area, I'm not alone, and there's a demand from diners with the disposable income to dine out regularly who give a shit about what they eat, where it comes from, and paying workers a living wage. People will pay for that kind of experience here; they understand the costs behind what's on the plate.

We live in a time when many chefs of different ethnic heritages—including relatively recent immigrants—are exploring a more diverse definition of what it means to be American, an American chef, and to serve American food. I'm delighted to be part of that continuing conversation.

CUCUMBER RAITA

Makes 4 cups

1 English cucumber, unpeeled

2 teaspoon yellow mustard seeds

1 teaspoon Toasted Cumin
 (see recipe page 25)

2 teaspoons salt

3 cups whole milk Greek yogurt
 (we use Straus)

This common Indian condiment made with yogurt is a welcome cooling accompaniment to many JBC dishes. The mustard seeds give it a slight horseradish-y taste. It's best made two or three hours in advance of serving so the mustard seeds have time to flavor the yogurt. Grating the cucumber and using a thick Greek yogurt make the texture smooth and luxurious.

Wash the cucumber thoroughly and grate on the largest holes of a box grater. Strain the excess liquid from the grated cucumber. In a spice grinder, pulse the mustard seeds to crack them open. Fold the grated cucumber with the cumin, mustard, salt, and yogurt and mix thoroughly. Store in an airtight container in the refrigerator for up to 3 days.

KACHUMBER SALAD

Makes 2 cups

1 medium fennel bulb

3 large carrots, peeled

3 celery stalks

1 bunch radish

2 lemons, juiced

1 tablespoon Toasted Cumin
 (see recipe page 25)

1 teaspoon salt

When I was growing up, my family was never much into leafy salads. Maybe it was the lack of lettuces (aside from iceberg) in Ohio, or just that green salads are not traditional to Indian cuisine. If we did have a salad at dinnertime, it was Kachumber, a basic chopped salad of crunchy veggies lightly dressed with lemon and cumin. This recipe is a riff on that salad, with some decidedly non-Indian additions like fresh fennel and celery. At the restaurant, we serve this simple salad as a side dish alongside our curries, with our Cucumber Raita and Spicy Apple Pickle.

Dice all the vegetables into bite-size pieces. Toss them with the lemon juice, cumin, and salt. Serve.

SPICY APPLE PICKLE

Makes 1 quart

6 Granny Smith apples
¼ cup fresh lemon juice
2 tablespoons mustard oil
  (buy at an Indian grocery store)
1 teaspoon turmeric powder
1 teaspoon Indian red chili powder
¼ cup Pickle Masala
  (see recipe page 111)
2 teaspoons salt

As a kid, I never really understood the allure of a raw mango pickle. It was just too sour and bitter for my tastes. Over time I have come to see its supporting role in a meal and appreciate its boldness. That said, I wanted to create a similar flavor profile that might be a little more accessible to a wider audience—including me. Granny Smith apples have a significant tartness—just like raw mango—but with less bitterness and a bit more residual sugar for a more balanced taste. I think my recipe has a similar essence to raw mango pickles but with a little less bite.

Quarter the apples and remove their cores. Cut the apples into a ½-inch dice. Toss the apples with the remaining ingredients, making sure all the ingredients are fully incorporated. Refrigerate in an airtight container for at least 24 hours. These pickles will keep for about 2 weeks in a fridge.

TURMERIC LEMON RICE

Serves 6

3 cups basmati rice
1 teaspoon turmeric powder
2 teaspoons salt
2 tablespoons fresh lemon juice
½ tablespoon neutral oil

This recipe is for the rice we make with all of our curries at JBC. The rice is a basic dish, but we give it a little oomph and visual appeal with added flavor and color from the lemon and turmeric. When I make rice at home, I use ghee for extra flavor, but at the restaurant we use neutral oil so that our rice works for vegans, too. Soaking the rice is a crucial step that many people do not realize helps it cook evenly.

Measure the rice into a shallow bowl. Fill the bowl with water to cover by at least 1 inch, and let the rice sit for 20 minutes. Strain the excess water and set it aside. In a medium saucepan combine the turmeric, salt, lemon juice, and oil. (Or substitute ghee for the oil if you'd prefer. See recipe page 22.) Add the soaked rice and cover it with cold water. The water should come up to about 1 inch from the top of the rice. Stir to dissolve the turmeric, place the saucepan on high heat, and bring the water to a boil. Watch the rice carefully. When the water has evaporated to the level of the surface of the rice, cover the pot and reduce the heat to low. Let the rice cook untouched for 15 minutes. After 15 minutes, uncover and check the rice for doneness. Tilt the pot slightly to see if any excess water remains. If there's extra water, return the rice to the heat for a few more minutes. Fluff the rice with a fork or rice paddle before serving. Store the rice in the refrigerator and use within 2 days.

GARAM MASALA CHICKPEAS

Serves 6

2 cups dried chickpeas

2 tablespoons neutral oil

1 yellow onion, julienned

1 tablespoon ginger, minced

1 tablespoon garlic, minced

1 tablespoon serrano chiles, minced

¼ cup JBC Garam Masala
(see recipe page 103)

2 tablespoons tomato paste

2 cups canned whole tomatoes

1 bunch lacinato kale, julienned
(also called dinosaur or
Tuscan kale)

Channa masala or chole is a curry house staple. Our version is not so far from the traditional dish. My only gripe with the original: It always seemed a bit too sweet. So we boost the spice of the dish with the addition of dark winter greens. Whenever I eat this dish, I feel like I am filling my body with healthy, earthy goodness.

Soak the chickpeas in cold water for at least 6 hours, ideally overnight. After soaking, drain the chickpeas. Heat the oil on medium high in a heavy-bottom saucepan for about 2 minutes. Add the onion and stir; the onion will begin to soften and become translucent after a few minutes. After about 5 minutes, add the ginger, garlic, and chiles and continue to stir. When the aromatics begin to brown slightly, add the garam masala and tomato paste. Stir to incorporate the tomato paste. Add the tomatoes and 1 cup of water; use a spoon to scrape any bits that stick to the bottom of the pot. Increase the heat to high and add the chickpeas. When the liquid comes to a boil, reduce the heat to medium and fold in the kale. Stir well and simmer on low for about 30 minutes. The chickpeas should be just cooked through. Taste-test them for doneness. Season to taste and serve with rice and raita.

HOLI, JBC STYLE

As timing would have it, we opened JBC right around the time of the Hindu spring festival known as Holi. It's also called the Festival of Colors and the Festival of Sharing Love.

Holi is my kind of celebration: playful, colorful, an opportunity to appreciate the end of winter and welcome spring. It also signifies the victory of good forces over evil. We could all use some of that right now. And everyone is fair game: You chase folks around and toss vivid dried powders at them.

Half the fun of Holi is setting up for the event. At JBC we use *thalis*, shallow stainless steel bowls we bought on our last trip to India, and fill them with striking blue, green, purple, pink, yellow, orange, and red powders. That part of the festivities—the color-flinging part—takes place in the parking lot in front of the restaurant when we have a critical mass.

It's an equal-opportunity event: young and old, friends and strangers, gay and straight, regulars and newcomers, rich and poor. Attendees are encouraged to wear all white for maximum color impact. It's a free-for-all, a carnival of colors, a chance to channel your inner child. It's also a way we give thanks for another year under our belts and thank our community for supporting our restaurant. The profit margins are razor thin in our industry; we don't take our customers for granted. We have a pani puri stand outside and a table full of Desi Jacks and other hearty snacks laid out for free inside. The spread might include hot dogs, fried chicken, masala potatoes, and other comforting fare. Revelers are encouraged to kick back over a beer or cocktail. We skip the religious aspects and focus on the fun.

We celebrated our fourth Holi Event in 2017. Each one is a little bigger than the last. We crank some tunes—maybe some hip-hop courtesy of Missy Elliot and Outkast, and a little early Motown Michael Jackson. These days the festivities take place right after brunch service. That's Holi, JBC style.

SUMMER EGGPLANT CURRY

Serves 6

1 globe eggplant
½ cup neutral oil
3 pounds mixed various eggplants
¼ cup JBC Garam Masala
    (see recipe page 103)
1 yellow onion, julienned
1 tablespoon ginger, minced
1 tablespoon garlic, minced
1 tablespoon serrano chiles, minced
2 tablespoons Dhanna Jeeru Masala
    (see recipe page 102)
1 teaspoon turmeric powder
2 tablespoons tomato paste
2 cups fresh diced tomatoes
    (use canned if unavailable)
1 bunch mustard greens,
    julienned
salt

This recipe is similar to the traditional globe eggplant dish called *baigan bartha*, a roasted and mashed spicy eggplant purée. I wanted to create a dish that encapsulated that flavor but also had some different textures in the mix. This is a summer dish, when a large variety of eggplants are abundant. We use what's called "toybox mix": a variety of heirloom eggplants such as Italian Rosa Bianca, long skinny Japanese, small round Indian, petite Thai green, and the tiny fairytale eggplants that are the size of a pinkie finger. By keeping the heirloom eggplants mostly intact and combining them with puréed globe eggplant, we can see and appreciate all these vegetables' textures and flavors.

Preheat the oven to 350°F. Cut the globe eggplant down the center from top to bottom, taking care to keep the stem intact. Rub it with salt and 1 tablespoon of the oil. Place the eggplant on a baking sheet lined with parchment paper or aluminum foil cut side down and roast it in the oven for 20 to 30 minutes. The eggplant skin will be pliable and soft to the touch when it is fully cooked. Remove the eggplant from the oven and let it cool.

When it is cool to the touch, scoop out the flesh and set it aside.

Cut the heirloom eggplants into bite-size pieces. Toss them with ¼ cup of the oil, the garam masala, and a pinch of salt. Roast them in the oven for 15 to 20 minutes until they are soft but still intact. Remove them from the oven and set them aside.

Heat a heavy-bottom saucepan on medium heat with the remaining oil. Add the onions and a pinch of salt and cook until the onions are translucent, about 3 minutes. Add the ginger, garlic, and chiles, stir and cook for about 3 minutes. Add the dhanna jeeru masala, turmeric, and tomato paste, and continue to stir for about 2 minutes. Add the tomatoes and 1 cup of water, increase the heat to high, and simmer for about 10 minutes. Season with salt to taste. Wilt the greens into the tomato sauce—about 5 minutes. Fold in the eggplant purée and roasted eggplants, simmer for 5 minutes. Serve with turmeric lemon rice.

COCONUT TAMARIND CURRY

Makes 6 servings

3 tablespoons coriander seeds

1 tablespoon cumin seeds

1 tablespoon brown mustard seeds

½ tablespoon green cardamom pods

½ cup neutral oil

½ yellow onion, julienned

6 fresh curry leaves

1 teaspoon fenugreek seeds

1 tablespoon salt

½ tablespoon garlic, minced

½ tablespoon ginger, minced

½ tablespoon serrano chiles, minced

3 tablespoons Tamarind Paste
   (see recipe page 23)

¼ teaspoon turmeric powder

1 can coconut milk
   (we use Chaokoh brand)

2 cups butternut squash, cut into
   1-inch cubes

2 cups mushrooms, sliced

1 bunch rainbow chard, julienned

Lush and tangy, this coconut curry sauce is loaded with fall vegetables like butternut squash, rainbow chard, and mushrooms. The earthy sweetness of the vegetables is a terrific balance to the sour tamarind-spiked sauce. Coconut milk is a simple way to add creamy richness to a vegetable curry while keeping it vegan. The sauce on its own works with fish or other seafood as well.

Preheat the oven to 350°F. Combine the coriander, cumin, and mustard seeds and cardamom pods on a sheet pan. Toast them for 5 to 7 minutes until the spices begin to smoke a bit and turn a little brown. Remove the spices from the oven and set them aside to cool. When they are fully cooled, grind them in a spice grinder in batches, until all the spices are fully ground.

Heat ¼ cup of the oil in a medium saucepan on medium high. Add the onions, curry leaves, and fenugreek seeds and stir. Season with salt. The curry leaves will crackle. When the onions begin to turn translucent—about 3 minutes—add the garlic, ginger, and chiles. In a measuring cup combine the tamarind paste with 3 tablespoons of warm water, and mix to soften and dissolve the paste. Continue stirring the saucepan for about 2 minutes, and then add the ground spice blend and turmeric. Stir the spices into the saucepan and let it all cook for about 2 minutes—the spices will begin to stick to the bottom of the pan. Pour in the tamarind and coconut milk and scrape the bottom of the pan to release any sticking spices. Bring the mixture to a boil and then lower the heat to simmer for about 5 minutes. Taste and season with more salt if needed.

Place the squash in a small saucepan with cold water. Bring the water to a boil, then reduce the heat to simmer for about 7 to 10 minutes. Drain the squash when it is cooked. Heat a large saucepan on medium with the remaining oil. Add the mushrooms, and stir to let the mushrooms brown, for about 3 minutes. Add the chard and squash and stir to lightly wilt the greens. After the greens begin to wilt, add the sauce and simmer for 5 minutes. Serve with turmeric lemon rice.

CURRY LEAF CORIANDER SHRIMP CURRY

Makes 6 servings

½ cup unsalted butter

12 fresh curry leaves

2 tablespoons ginger, minced

2 tablespoons Dhanna Jeeru Masala
   (see recipe page 102)

4 cups puréed canned tomatoes

2 tablespoons salt

1 tablespoon Indian red chili powder

2 tablespoons neutral oil

2 pounds wild-caught shrimp,
   peeled and deveined

2 cups green peas

This is an easy yet satisfying curry to make. It might be a simple dish, but the sauce is so scrumptious I sometimes just have it over rice on its own. We source sustainable, wild-caught shrimp from the Gulf of Mexico. In the spring, fresh peas are plentiful; at times of the year when peas are out of season, we substitute frozen organic peas. Humble and comforting, this dish could quickly become a welcome addition to a weekly repertoire.

Melt the butter in a heavy-bottom, medium saucepan on medium heat. When the butter is fully melted and begins to foam slightly, add the curry leaves and ginger. The curry leaves will crackle a bit. After about 2 minutes, add the masala and stir for another 2 minutes to cook the spices. Add the tomatoes, salt, and red chili powder. Scrape the bottom of the pan to release any ginger or spices that may have stuck to the bottom. Taste and add more salt if necessary. Set the sauce aside.

Heat the oil in a nonstick sauté pan on high. Add the shrimp and let it brown on one side. Turn the shrimp over to brown the other side. Pour the warm sauce on top of the shrimp, and then add the peas. Simmer for about 3 to 5 minutes to ensure the shrimp are cooked all the way through. Serve with turmeric lemon rice.

FENUGREEK CHICKEN CURRY

Makes 6 servings

For the marinade:

2 cups whole plain yogurt

½ cup garlic, minced

½ cup ginger, minced

2 tablespoons JBC Garam Masala
   (see recipe page 103)

1 teaspoon turmeric powder

2 tablespoons salt

6 chicken legs, skin removed
   and cut into pieces

For the curry:

1 cup unsalted butter

2 yellow onions, julienned

2 red bell pepper, julienned

½ cup ginger, minced

½ cup garlic, minced

2 tablespoons serrano chiles, minced

1 cup fresh fenugreek leaves,
   roughly chopped

1 teaspoon turmeric

3 tablespoons Dhanna Jeeru
   Masala (see recipe page 102)

3 tablespoons JBC Garam Masala
   (see recipe page 103)

2 quarts diced Early Girl or
   San Marzano tomatoes

¼ cup heavy whipping cream

I especially like serving this curry in the summer when we have fresh Early Girl or San Marzano tomatoes from local farms like Dirty Girl and Full Belly. These are great sauce tomatoes that add a deep richness to this curry. The fresh fenugreek leaves really make this dish sing, contributing earthy, classically Indian flavor notes. Substitute frozen or dried leaves if fresh fenugreek isn't available. But be warned: the flavors will be muted in comparison. This dish tastes best when the chicken is marinated overnight. I prefer to use chicken legs because of how well they braise. If you are using a whole chicken, add the breast meat halfway through the braising process to avoid overcooking the meat.

To marinate the chicken:

Combine the yogurt, garlic, ginger, masala, turmeric, and salt. Cover the chicken legs in the marinade and refrigerate them for at least 2 hours, ideally overnight.

To make the sauce:

Melt the butter in a large, heavy-bottom saucepan on medium heat. Add the onions and bell peppers, and season them with salt to soften. After about 5 minutes, add the other aromatics: the ginger, garlic, chiles, and fenugreek. Stir for about 3 minutes to incorporate them, then add the turmeric and masalas. Continue stirring to keep the spices from sticking to the bottom of the pot and cook for about 3 minutes. Add the diced tomatoes and use the juices to scrape any spices from the bottom of the pan and incorporate them into the sauce.

Bring the liquid to a boil, then lower the heat to a simmer. Add the marinated chicken legs; make sure they are fully submerged in the liquid. Cover and let them simmer for about 20 minutes. Check the chicken legs for doneness: the meat should easily pull away from the bone. When the chicken is fully cooked, stir in the cream. Serve over turmeric lemon rice.

LAMB KOFTA

Makes 6 servings

For the lamb sauce:

2 pounds boneless leg
   (or shoulder) of lamb

3 tablespoons neutral oil

1 yellow onion, julienned

2 tablespoons ginger, minced

2 tablespoons serrano chiles, minced

¼ cup Smoky Black Cardamom Masala
   (see recipe page 104)

4 cups whole canned tomatoes

1 tablespoon salt

For the kofta:

6 duck eggs

1 pound ground lamb

1 tablespoon ginger, minced

1 tablespoon serrano chiles, minced

2 tablespoons Kheema Masala
   (see recipe page 106)

2 teaspoons salt

1 egg white (reserve yolk
   for future use)

1 cup plain all-purpose flour

From the moment Juhu Beach Club was conceived I wanted to put an Indian version of a Scotch egg on the menu. That classic dish—a hard-boiled egg wrapped inside a sausage, coated in breadcrumbs, and deep-fried—is a UK standard. While I was busy testing different versions of this recipe, my lovely wife Ann researched the origins of the dish. She discovered something that surprised and delighted us both: It turns out that Nargisi Kofta, an Indian dish, predates the Scotch egg by a century. The kofta featured a hard-boiled egg wrapped in lamb and simmered in a tomato sauce rich with spices. Ann's find sparked a sharp turn in my creative process. The deep-fried starter Scotch Egg was off the table and in its place was Lamb Kofta, a saucy, meaty entrée. Several steps can be prepped a day in advance. This is a statement dish to serve at a dinner party or special family gathering.

Preheat the oven to 300°F. Trim the excess fat from the lamb leg or shoulder—or ask a butcher to do it in advance. Cut the lamb into 2-inch pieces, and season them all over with salt. Heat the oil in a large, heavy-bottom saucepan on high. When the oil is just about to start smoking, begin adding the lamb pieces in one even layer. Using a pair of tongs, turn the lamb pieces to evenly brown them on all sides. Remove the lamb when the meat is fully browned—in about 7 to 10 minutes. Set the meat aside in a medium casserole.

(recipe continues)

Keep the saucepan on the heat and add the onions. Season the onions with a pinch of salt and stir them to release any browned bits from the bottom of the pan. When the onions begin to soften—about 3 minutes—add 2 tablespoons each of the ginger, chiles, and masala. Stir the onions to fully incorporate the aromatics. After about 3 minutes, add the tomatoes and stir to scrape all the browned bits off the bottom of the pan. Use the spoon to break up the tomatoes. Season the mixture with salt to taste, and pour the sauce over the browned lamb. Cut a piece of parchment paper big enough to cover the top of the casserole and press it onto the surface of the lamb in the sauce. Cover the casserole tightly with a lid or aluminum foil and place it in the oven.

After 3 hours, remove the lamb from the oven and check it for doneness. The meat should easily pull apart. If the lamb is not fully cooked, return it to the oven for up to another half hour. Set it aside to cool.

Bring a large saucepan of water to a boil. When the water is boiling, lower in the duck eggs for 6 minutes. Fill a bowl big enough for the eggs with ice water. Remove the cooked eggs from the heat and plunge them into the ice water immediately. When they are cooled—about 10 minutes—peel them and set them aside.

Mix the ground lamb with the ginger, chiles, masala, and salt. Add the egg white to the lamb and mix it in with your hands to fully incorporate. Divide the lamb into 6 equal portions. Using two pieces of plastic wrap, place one portion of lamb directly onto the plastic and place another piece of plastic on top of the lamb mixture. Flatten the lamb into rounds about ½-inch thick. Peel off the plastic wrap, and place one egg in the middle of the flattened round. Wrap the lamb around the duck egg to fully encase the egg. Set the ball aside and repeat with the remaining eggs. Chill all six lamb-wrapped eggs in the refrigerator for up to a day.

Remove the braised lamb from the liquid and reserve the liquid. Shred the braised lamb using two forks, or by hand. Skim the braising liquid to remove the excess fat from the top of the pan. Return the shredded, braised lamb to the braising liquid and set it aside.

Increase the oven temperature to 350°F. Place the flour into a medium bowl, and gently toss the lamb-wrapped eggs in the flour—one by one—and shake each one to remove any excess flour. Place the lamb-wrapped eggs on a sheet pan with a fitted rack to slightly elevate the eggs. Bake this in the oven for 5 to 10 minutes, until the meat is just set around the egg. Bring the shredded lamb and sauce to a simmer in a large casserole, and nestle the browned eggs in the sauce.

Serve each egg with a ladle of braised lamb sauce on top of turmeric lemon rice.

landed on *Top Chef* in 2009: season six, Las Vegas. It was an honor and a privilege: there were sixteen other chefs from all over the country, many with their own restaurants, fine dining pedigrees, James Beard awards. It was a pretty impressive, and intimidating, group.

It was also like high school and not in a good way: cliques, bro culture. It was not my scene. I lasted three episodes, eliminated over a pasta salad. It was painful, but also a relief: I was not having fun. And then I had to come back for the finale and serve as an assistant to one of the finalists. I was so bummed when my name was randomly chosen. I just wanted the whole nightmare to be over.

In retrospect, I should have prepared in advance for the competition. I was naïve. *Top Chef* is not the kind of competition where you can wing it, improvise on the fly. You need to have your dishes down and tweak them as circumstances dictate. It was a tough lesson to learn in a very public forum. And there's really no way to prepare yourself for the amount of attention—both positive and negative—that comes with such wide-ranging exposure.

That season—the program has run for fourteen years—is still considered one of the strongest crews of professional cooks to ever compete in the reality show's history. It's also the only season of this Bravo series to win an Emmy.

It was beyond humiliating. I suffered through several weeks of abject despair. But the old saw really is true: Failure is a necessary part of success. If you're not willing to put yourself out there, knowing that you could mess up big time, then you're likely not growing or learning anything as a person and as a professional. Sometimes you have to push yourself outside of your comfort zone to reach your goals.

I like to joke that if there was an award handed out years later for the person who bridged the greatest chasm between how poorly they did on their season of *Top Chef* and how well they did in their *actual* career, I might take that honor.

But I wouldn't be keeping it real if before the ecstasy of success, I didn't come clean about the agony of failure. Failure and I go way back.

So there was that farfalle with canned artichokes and jarred sun-dried tomatoes on a military base in Texas. Neither *Top Chef* presenter Padma Lakshmi or judge Tom Colicchio cared for it. On the episode before, Tom wasn't impressed with how I struggled to open clams. But what they didn't show viewers was that although I might have been slow and had terrible technique, I got the job done. I prised those little fuckers open.

After getting axed early, I felt horrible, in the darkest place of my life. *Top Chef* didn't make me look like an asshole or a jerk. But it did make me look clueless. I looked like I didn't know what I was doing or how to cook. I'm a gregarious extrovert by nature, but on that show I looked tentative, overshadowed by insecurity. No professional chef wants that reminder available on Netflix for anyone to watch anytime. Thankfully, my chosen family had my back: they didn't care about the damn TV show.

But San Francisco is a pretty small town in many ways. I found myself not wanting to go out in public places once the show first aired—especially to industry spots: restaurants, bars, cafés—my typical sanctuaries.

The restaurant world is a high-profile, high-stakes environment. The industry is only just starting to talk about the pressures that come with the job and the stress, anxiety, depression, self-medicating, and poor self-care that are rampant in the business. Everyone's

a food critic these days—from a random diner on Yelp to the casual TV food show watcher. We are constantly being judged, and every plate coming out of our kitchen matters.

When the program first aired, I was working for the food service provider Bon Appétit Management Company, running the largest café at Google's main campus in Mountain View.

While the management higher-ups at BAMCO, as it's called for short, stood by me (I'd been with the company for four years), my poor showing on such a high-profile show was embarrassing to my bosses at Google. I was keenly aware of that. I also had to suck it up. I had a job to do. Did I cry my eyes out when I drove home from work? Yes.

But I was also in charge of overseeing 120 people. I had to keep it together at work, no matter how I felt inside. And, trust me, I felt bad. I wanted to run away.

I was also commuting long hours to the suburbs to a job where I wasn't cooking, and there was a lot of politics. I wanted out. Ann and I don't have kids or a mortgage. So why stay in something that was killing my soul—even if to some it might be considered a dream job? I needed to go figure out what I wanted to do professionally that would bring me joy. So I resigned.

That's when I came up with the idea for Juhu Beach Club.

As successful as we've been with JBC, we've had our missteps. You have to screw up sometimes, take risks, to figure out what works. After JBC opened, we tried doing lunch. It didn't make sense in this neighborhood. We also tried a hot dog window at the restaurant in the summer and, later, a pav stand in San Francisco at the Ferry Building Farmers Market Plaza. Both proved short-lived experiments. We found ourselves stretched too thin. So we pulled the plug. We were courted by an investor in Hong Kong; we opened a JBC satellite there in 2015 that lasted only nine months. Turns out keeping on top of an international outpost is too big a juggle for our small team—especially for a chef like me who wants to control everything from where the spices are sourced to how bright the lights are at any given time during service.

We have a new venture in 2017: Navi Kitchen, not far from JBC. It's a casual undertaking—Indian-accented pizza and masala-rubbed rotisserie chicken. We're hoping we've hit on a winning formula, but we've also learned when to cut our losses. We try stuff. That's what Ann and I like to do. We're entrepreneurial in that way, calculated risk takers.

⸻

Back in 2002, Ann got an opportunity to move to London for a big job. We decided to go. Ann kept saying: "You should go to culinary school." We landed in London on March 15, 2002, and I started school at Le Cordon Bleu on March 18.

It was my first time living in London since I'd left at age five. We both loved it. London is a huge city, full of fabulous history and architecture, over-the-top fashion, and people from all over the world. But Ann was also traveling a lot for work. The first year we were there I used to joke that I'd moved to London, but Ann lived on planes, in airports, and at hotel rooms— and she'd visit me on occasion, when her crushing work schedule allowed. It was lonely at times, though I was fortunate to have family friends to visit on weekends, an hour's tube ride away from our flat in Central London.

And at culinary school, I had a lot to learn. My classmates knew more about European cuisine and classic French culinary techniques than I did, like turning

potatoes, deboning quail, and all sorts of pastry that I had no experience with at all. Once again, insecurity, an outsider complex, and an imposter syndrome bubbled to the surface—all of it.

I was a decent home cook. But I felt out of my league in culinary school. I was always playing catch-up. A lot of the students at Le Cordon Bleu just had way more exposure to fine dining and more experience cooking than I had. While I struggled the first few months, I eventually found my groove and made a few great friends.

My externship, which you do at the end of the yearlong program, was at the five-star Claridge's Hotel. I was

assigned to banqueting. Terrifying. You're making fancy little canapés for high-profile guests like Tom Hanks and Naomi Campbell. My boss was four years younger than me but had been working in a kitchen since he was sixteen. He was just ruthless. I was miserable—again.

In culinary school I could never properly quenelle anything. It's a technique where you form something into an oval shape. So of course, one of the first things my boss said to me was: "You're going to quenelle this goat cheese with these two tiny teaspoons." This guy stood over me, kind of intimidating. But, low and behold, all of a sudden I could do it. I learned early that performing well under pressure is part of professional cooking.

There was this older Indian man who made all the tea sandwiches at the hotel. He did this one job all day, and he'd probably been doing it for twenty years. There was a clear distinction between this middle-aged brown man, who was never going to advance professionally, and these young, white, mostly working-class British kids who were on track for a culinary career. They looked down on him. That kind of attitude was widespread. It infuriated me. One day he tried doing something a little differently, and his superiors jumped all over him. It was awful to witness.

That was one of my early experiences of racism in the kitchen. I got schooled quickly in traditional restaurant hierarchy. It was so disappointing.

I also loathed the ego-driven chefs who had tantrums or who got in underlings' faces, all of that negativity in military-style, hierarchical, professional kitchens. It wasn't fun. They—and it must be said, they were mostly men— were constantly power tripping, and they created a culture of fear in the kitchen. So much for my idealistic goal of making food with love!

I didn't want to work in that type of environment. But it was like an aggressive cancer: widespread and mutating everywhere. I landed a *stage*—that's an unpaid internship—at the acclaimed independent restaurant Moro. I was psyched: The chefs were ex–River Café people, these places had a similar sensibility to the Northern California ethos I was drawn to—local, seasonal, sustainable, organic. I loved the environment: a small, bustling kitchen of diverse and smart cooks. Culturally it was a good fit. But I didn't get the job after the stage. My skill level wasn't where it needed to be. I felt rejected and ashamed. Was I ever going to succeed in a professional kitchen?

I didn't know it then, but it was the start of me failing up. And you know what? My triumphs in the profession are that much sweeter because of the stumbles and pivots and screwups along the way.

Eventually I landed an actual job. I was the only woman in the kitchen at Peter Gordon's esteemed Sugar Club in Soho. It was a hot spot in its day. He's a celebrated New Zealand chef. When I worked there, the head chef was an Aussie, David Selex; he fostered a supportive environment. It was an almost all-male but ethnically diverse kitchen: Australian, New Zealander, Venezuelan, Ecuadorian, Japanese, and me, the young Indian American with a bald head. It was a great experience. There was this camaraderie in the kitchen. They embraced me. Sometimes I think the diversity of the staff was part of why it worked: No one group dominated. They cursed and were coarse and vulgar, but they were so funny and there was genuine respect. The menu was contemporary fine dining with global reach: I made a ton of kangaroo salads. We served sashimi, deep-fried tofu in *dashi*, smoked goat cheese with chili jam and roasted beets.

That's where I learned you could have a good time *and* do a good job *and* plate beautiful food in a professional kitchen.

We moved back to San Francisco in 2004. I staged at a bunch of big-name places, trying to get a foothold in a competitive food town. At one restaurant there was a screaming chef. I felt unsafe. I kept thinking: Is it possible to do it differently?

——————

Ever the contrarian, I figured, fuck it, if I can't find a work environment that feels right, I'll create my own. So Ann and I launched a boutique catering business, Saffron Hill. Ann was burnt out from her previous job and wanted to do something else. We offered contemporary Indian hors d'oeuvres for parties and events with 50 to 100 guests. We did it for about two years and even launched a line of curry sauces that we sold at local grocery stores. Then Ann decided she didn't want to lug dirty dishes around at one a.m. anymore. And it wasn't like we were making much money. She went back to building her career. I decided to get a salary gig, too. But I'd had a taste of what it was like to be my own boss.

Soon after, I landed the BAMCO job. The company provides corporate food service for businesses, universities, and museums. I started as the executive catering chef and after a year got bumped to executive chef of the de Young Museum and the Legion of Honor in San Francisco. From there I did a short stint at the now-closed Acme Chophouse, near the Giants ballpark. And then like I mentioned, I moved on to serve as the executive chef at the largest Google cafeteria at the company's Mountain View headquarters—it's called Charlie's Cafe—when I appeared on *Top Chef*.

Meanwhile, it was an exciting time food-wise in San Francisco: Food carts, food trucks, and underground supper clubs were popping up everywhere. It was this avant-garde, happening moment, cooks of all kinds were experimenting with a wide range of cuisines. I wanted to be a part of it.

That's when I came up with the name Juhu Beach Club and the idea to do Indian food . . . *my* Indian food. It's funny because now I own an "Indian" restaurant and find myself championing a cuisine and culture that I spent a lot of my early adult life rejecting. I've always felt like an outsider: a lesbian, a person of color, an Indian American who doesn't speak Hindi. It's ironic that now I champion the cuisine of my cultural heritage.

I've always been a rebel at heart. I like to mix things up, spice things up, keep things fresh. I'm a bit of a cowboy in the kitchen. I've come to celebrate being different, unexpected, a person with an alternative point of view. I've done okay for myself failing up in the kitchen.

In the fall of 2016 I had a TV redemption of sorts. Juhu Beach Club was featured on culinary provocateur

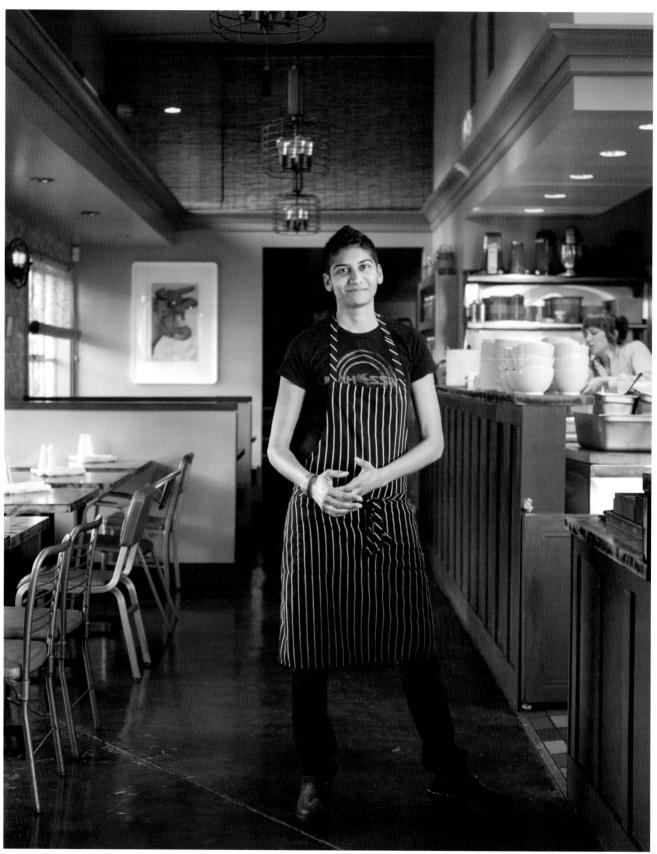

Anthony Bourdain's CNN series *Parts Unknown*. Oakland food writer John Birdsall served as the TV host's on-the-ground guide. I'm grateful to John for including me in a list of innovative restaurants in Oakland for the program's producers to scout.

The producers picked JBC as one of the places Tony, as he goes by, would visit. So we fed Tony and John that night, while the cameras rolled. And then after that was over, we fed the crew. Of course, we fed the crew.

A few months after shooting I watched the show at home with Ann and friends. I wasn't sure what to expect. Given my previous national TV exposure, I was nervous.

Turns out, I needn't have been. On the segment, about halfway into the show, there's Tony and John eating at our restaurant bar while we chat. We served Bhel Salad, Manchurian Cauliflower, Chili Paneer, Fenugreek Chicken Curry, and Lamb Kofta. Tony described the food as "unassuming but utterly delicious . . . the food is both familiar and uniquely her own."

If that's not failing up, I don't know what is.

SASSY LASSI

Makes a half-gallon pitcher

1 can mango pulp (available
    at Asian grocers and
    select markets)
1 quart whole plain yogurt
6 limes, juiced
1 cup cold water
½ tablespoon Toasted Cumin
    (see recipe page 25)
1 teaspoon salt

As much as I love mango, I've never really enjoyed the mango lassis I've tried at traditional Indian restaurants. They always taste too cloyingly sweet for my palate. The JBC mango lassi is not supersweet. There's no added sugar—the sweetness comes courtesy of the fruit: mango pulp and lime juice. A generous amount of salt results in a drink that's a balance of sweet, salty, and tart.

Combine all the ingredients in a bowl and whisk to fully incorporate them. Pour the mixture into a pitcher and serve over ice. Store in the refrigerator and use within 3 days.

NIMBU PANI
(AKA INDIAN-ACCENTED LEMONADE)

Makes a half-gallon pitcher

2 cups Simple Syrup
   (recipe follows, page 254)
2 cups cold water
4 cups fresh lemon juice
½ tablespoon black salt
½ tablespoon Toasted Cumin
   (see recipe page 25)
½ bunch fresh cilantro, roughly
   chopped

A Puerto Rican friend of mine once told me Puerto Ricans like their food so sweet they put sugar in their orange juice. I countered that Indians like savory food so much my parents put salt and cumin in their OJ. That was my starting point for this lemonade. Street stalls sell Nimbu Pani, which literally means "lime water," all over Mumbai. Note: This lemonade is also fabulous with vodka or gin, see below.

Combine the simple syrup with the water, lemon juice, salt, and cumin. Stir well. Set the pitcher of lemonade aside in the refrigerator.

In a blender combine the cilantro with enough water to barely cover the herbs. Blend until the cilantro is fully puréed. Serve the lemonade over ice with a drizzle of cilantro water on top.

Desi Drop (Nimbu Pani variation)

Makes 1 cocktail

2 ounces gin or vodka
   (brand of choice)
4 ounces Nimbu Pani
   (see recipe page 253)
1 teaspoon cilantro water
   (see recipe page 253)
Fresh cilantro

One of our most popular cocktails, the Desi Drop is a grown-up variation on the Nimbu Pani.

In a cocktail shaker combine the spirit with the lemonade and fill the shaker with ice. Shake the drink to fully chill the ingredients. Strain the drink into a coupe or martini glass, drizzle it with the cilantro water, and garnish it with fresh cilantro leaves.

Simple Syrup

Makes 2 quarts

6 cups granulated sugar
6 cups water

Many of our drinks use simple syrup as a sweetener. This is a basic 1:1 ratio syrup that works for boozy beverages or nonalcoholic drinks.

In a saucepan combine the sugar and water, and heat them on medium. Whisk until all the sugar is fully dissolved. Remove the pan from the heat and let it cool. Keep the simple syrup in an airtight container in the refrigerator for up to 2 weeks.

SEX ON JUHU BEACH

Makes 6 drinks

½ cup dried cranberries
¼ teaspoon Chai Masala
  (see recipe page 111)
¼ cup granulated sugar
12 ounces white rum
  (brand of choice)
1 cup mango pulp
1½ cups lime juice, freshly squeezed
½ cup Simple Syrup
  (see recipe page 254)
orange, lime, and/or lemon wedge
  (as garnish)

This drink really started as a joke. It is in fact loosely based on the college frat party concoction Sex on the Beach. Unlike its namesake, this drink is actually pretty tasty. We serve it with white rum, but it works just as well with vodka. It's a party starter: Make a pitcher to share with a group.

Combine the dried cranberries, masala, and sugar with ½ cup of water in a small saucepan. Place the saucepan on medium-high heat. When the water begins to boil, reduce the heat to simmer and soften the cranberries. Remove the pan from the heat and let it cool. Transfer the mixture to a blender and purée.

In a pitcher combine the rum, mango pulp, lime juice, simple syrup, and cranberry purée with 1 cup of cold water. Fill the pitcher with ice and serve this drink with a glass garnished with orange, lime, and/or lemon wedges.

JBC MASALA CHAI

Makes 6 cups

5 black teabags
  (we use PG Tips brand)
⅓ cup granulated sugar
½ tablespoon Chai Masala
  (see recipe page 111)
½ tablespoon fresh ginger, minced
2 cups whole milk

In the past twenty years in the United States I have seen chai go from a drink enjoyed mostly in Indian households and restaurants to the beverage of choice at every corner café. We make our chai from scratch at the beginning of service with fresh ingredients and our own signature blend of spices. Many Indian customers say that it reminds them of their mother's or grandmother's recipe. I'll take the compliment.

Combine all the ingredients except for the milk with 2 cups of water in a medium saucepan, and heat them on high. When the water comes to a boil, add the milk and reduce the heat to medium. Let the liquid come to a simmer for about 5 minutes. Remove the pan from the heat and strain the solids. This drink can be chilled and served as iced chai. Use the chilled chai within 3 days.

High Chai

Makes 1 drink

2 ounces bourbon (brand of choice)
8 ounces hot chai

Pour the bourbon into a warm mug and top it with the hot chai.

Mai Chai

Makes 1 drink

2 ounces white rum (brand of choice)
10 ounces chilled chai

Fill a pint glass with ice. Pour the rum and cold chai over the ice.

BANDRA BANGRA

Makes 6 drinks

1½ cups Simple Syrup
  (see recipe page 254)
1 tablespoon ginger, minced
1½ cups lime juice, freshly squeezed
12 ounces bourbon (brand of choice)
soda water
1 lime, cut into wedges

This drink is named after Bandra, a hipster neighborhood in Mumbai that is synonymous with fun—an area of boutiques, cafés, and bars frequented by a growing middle-class millennial demographic. We think Temescal, where JBC is located, is also pretty cool, so we borrowed the name.

Combine the simple syrup and ginger in a small saucepan on high heat. When the liquid comes to a boil, remove the pan from the heat, cover it, and let it steep for at least 5 hours. After steeping, strain out the ginger, and mix in the lime juice. To make the drink, fill a collins glass (or other tall tumbler) with ice. In a cocktail shaker combine ice, 2 ounces of bourbon per drink, and 4 ounces of the ginger-lime mixer. Pour into the collins glass. Top it off with soda water and garnish it with a lime wedge. Drinks can be made in batches, if needed.

BLOODY MEERA

Makes 6 drinks

2 dried chile de árbol

1 tablespoon yellow mustard seeds

1 tablespoon cumin seeds

½ cup white wine vinegar

¼ cup lemon juice, freshly squeezed

¼ cup lime juice, freshly squeezed

¼ cup garlic, minced

¼ cup ginger, minced

2 tablespoons serrano chiles,
   minced

1 cup cilantro stems

½ cup fresh fenugreek leaves

2 tablespoons salt

½ gallon canned tomato juice

12 ounces vodka (or gin),
   brand of choice

For the garnish:

6 stalks celery

6 pepperoncinis

6 fresh lemon wedges

In our version of the spicy universal hangover cure—the Bloody Mary—we forgo the horseradish and Worcestershire sauce for ginger and cilantro stems. If fresh fenugreek leaves aren't available, just omit them. I prefer to have my bloody with gin: give it a try; it's a refreshing change.

To make mixer:
Place the chiles, mustard seeds, cumin, and vinegar in a blender and pulse. Add the remaining ingredients except for the tomato juice and purée. Mix the puréed ingredients with the tomato juice. This mixture can keep in a pitcher in the refrigerator for up to 3 days.

To make the drink:
In a cocktail shaker combine 2 ounces vodka (or gin) with 6 ounces of mixer for each drink. Fill the shaker with ice and shake vigorously to chill and combine. Pour the drink into a pint glass full of ice. Garnish with the celery, pepperoncini, and lemon.

THE ELEPHANT'S FURY

Makes 8 drinks

¼ cup fresh turmeric root,
  roughly chopped
¾ cup granulated sugar
2 dried chiles de árbol
1 cup lime juice, freshly squeezed
¼ cup salt
¼ cup Indian red chili powder
1 lime for garnish
8 ounces mescal (brand of choice)
8 ounces tequila (brand of choice)

This cocktail was created by a JBC server, Liv, who has worked at the restaurant for several years. It's a winning combo of earthy turmeric, smoky mescal, citrus tartness, and a little chile heat at the finish. Substitute bourbon for mescal, if preferred.

Place the turmeric and ¼ cup of water in a blender and purée until smooth. In a small saucepan combine ¾ cup of water with the sugar and puréed turmeric and bring to a boil. Stir to dissolve the sugar as the water comes to a boil. Turn off the heat and let the liquid steep in the pot for at least 2 hours. After steeping, strain the solids by pouring the mixture through a sieve. Retain the liquid and compost the solids. Soften the dried chiles in a bowl in a small amount of warm water. Remove the chiles from the water and blend with ¼ cup of lime juice, and strain into the turmeric syrup. Add the remaining lime juice. Cool the mixer in the refrigerator until it is totally chilled, about 1 hour.

To make the drinks:
Combine the salt and chili powder on a small plate. Cut the limes into rounds and run a lime around the rim of each glass. Dip the rim of each glass into the salt and chili powder. Make the drinks one at a time in a cocktail shaker. Measure 1 ounce each of mescal and tequila into the shaker per cocktail. Add 2 ounces of the turmeric mixer and a few cubes of ice, and shake until the shaker is cold on the outside. Strain the drink into a salt-rimmed glass and garnish with a lime round.

SARI NOT SORRY

Makes 8 drinks

4 strawberries

1 tablespoon sugar

10 fresh mint sprigs

1½ cups Nimbu Pani (see recipe page 253)

2 teaspoons absinthe (brand of choice)

2 cups or 16 ounces bourbon (brand of choice)

This is a seasonal drink, since we don't have locally grown strawberries all year. This cocktail is a group front-of-house effort: Credit for this concoction goes to JBC server Liv; naming rights to server Sophie. We use a locally made absinthe from St. George Spirits.

To make the strawberry purée:

Cut the stems off the strawberries and combine them in a small saucepan with the sugar and ½ cup of water. Bring the water to a boil and simmer for 3 minutes, until the fruit is soft. Use a blender to purée the mixture until it is smooth. Pick 8 mint leaves for the garnish.

To make the drinks:

In a cocktail shaker, make the drinks one at a time. Place one mint sprig in the shaker and muddle it with an ice cube. Add 1½ ounces of Nimbu Pani, ½ ounce of the strawberry purée, 2 drops of absinthe, and 2 ounces of bourbon. Shake them until the cocktail shaker is cold on the outside. Strain the drink into a cocktail glass with a few ice cubes and garnish it with a mint leaf.

SMOKY NEGRONI

Makes 2 drinks

For the smoky cardamom tincture:
2 black cardamom pods crushed
½ cup Everclear
    (or other rectified spirit)

For the Negroni:
1½ ounces gin
1½ ounces Contratto Bitter
1½ ounces Contratto Rosato
3 drops smoky cardamom tincture
thin piece of orange peel,
    ½ inch in width

The Negroni served up is my go-to cocktail. Our version strays very little from the classic—aside from a bit of smoky spice, thanks to the black cardamom pods. Instead of big-brand labels, we use an all-natural bitter from Italy called Contratto Bitter. We use the company's Rosato Sweet Vermouth as well. The flavors are more balanced and less sugary than commonly known brands of bitter or vermouth, but, if needed, substitute these brands, which will work in a pinch. Heads-up: The tincture requires steeping for a couple of weeks.

To make the tincture:
Heat a dry pan on high with the two cardamom pods inside. Let them cook until they are smoking, about 2 minutes. Remove the pods from the pan and lightly crush them with the back of a pan. Place the crushed cardamom pods in a bottle or jar and pour the Everclear over them. Close the jar tightly and let the tincture steep for 2 weeks. Tincture will keep for 6 months.

To make the Negroni:
In a cocktail shaker combine all the ingredients except for the orange peel. Fill the shaker with ice and stir to chill and incorporate the ingredients. Run the orange peel around the outside rim of a chilled coupe or martini glass. Strain the drink into the glasses evenly and drop a piece of peel in each glass to garnish.

MONKEY MARGARITA

Makes 6 drinks

4 tablespoons Tamarind Paste
   (see recipe page 23)
4 tablespoons hot water
½ cup Simple Syrup
   (see recipe page 254)
1 cup lime juice, freshly squeezed
½ cup triple sec
2 tablespoons salt
2 tablespoons Indian red chili powder
1 lime, cut into wedges
12 ounces tequila

Deriving its tartness from fresh lime juice and tamarind, this margarita is a crowd pleaser. I recommend making it in a pitcher for a group to enjoy. The tartness of the tamarind gives the drink more tang than lime juice alone. And the salt-chile powder rim adds an unexpected twist.

To make the mixer:
Mix the tamarind with the hot water, and whisk them to fully dissolve the paste. Combine the tamarind mixture with the simple syrup, lime juice, and triple sec.

To make the drinks:
Mix the salt and chili powder on a flat plate. Run a lime wedge around the rim of each glass and dip the rim into the salt mixture.

Fill a cocktail shaker with 2 ounces of tequila and 4 ounces of the margarita mixer for each drink, top with ice, and shake vigorously. Strain the drink into the glasses and garnish each with a lime wedge.

Chapter Nine

MISTRY SOLVED

The proposal: It had been coming for a while. Ann was ready. I was ready. There were a number of times when she said: "I think I know what you're about to do and now is not the time." I know she didn't want some showy, grand gesture—no hot air balloon ride or expensive ring—but what to do?

I wanted to do something special, unique, us. So one Friday night at the end of July in 2014 I made Ann a green vegetable curry to have for dinner at home while I worked at the restaurant. And on the inside of the take-home container I wrote in black Sharpie: "Will you marry me?"

For whatever reason, she told me later that the smell of the curry in the car triggered such a strong nostalgic emotion for her that she found herself still sitting there long after she'd gotten home. It was the sort of thing that if a neighbor had noticed it might have seemed a bit bizarre. She was having a moment.

When she eventually got out of the car, she set down the bag of food and proceeded to tidy the house. Then she finally opened the box and saw what I'd written.

I'd almost forgotten I'd done it, as crazy as that sounds. It was a busy Friday night. I was on the line. I knew at the end of the night we'd have a chance to reconnect.

I'm juggling multiple orders, a packed house, in full JBC mode. I get a text. I grab my phone: it's from Ann. A photo. In red pen in little letters directly underneath what I had written on the curry container: "Yes!" It was adorable.

We'd been together for so long—almost twenty years—we'd talked about a wedding of some kind a million times. We're party throwers. We wanted a celebration—we also wanted our marriage to be legal, which is partly why we had waited.

We didn't want to fork over a lot of money on a lavish gala. Small and meaningful felt more our speed than a big wedding reception. We decided to do it fast and fun with our chosen family and friends in the summer, and then we did a celebratory dinner with our parents in December over the holidays, since they were coming to visit then anyway.

It felt like it was time to make this commitment to each other because we'd been through so much, especially in the past few years.

Friday, August 29, 2014, we went to City Hall in Oakland with close friends.

The marriage commissioner, a sweet Latina, cried. She was so happy for us—we could finally get married legally. When you get married at City Hall, it's like being in a conference waiting room and the service is over and done with in fifteen minutes. It's really not very romantic. But we made it festive, special, fun. I wore a bow tie with a white shirt and black pants. Ann had on an adorable, fitted, black-and-white dress. She made her own bouquet of crimson roses. Our friends Jill and Gretchen decorated Jill's car for the short drive following the ceremony. As we hopped in the back to leave, Jill cued up "Watch the Throne," a collaboration between Jay Z and Kanye West. That's one of our favorite albums. We drank champagne. It was a very good day.

That Sunday we threw a party in our backyard for about twenty of our closest friends. A three-piece jazz band played. I catered my own wedding. The JBC crew cooked. We had duck carnitas tacos with pickled carrots and jalapeños on the side, a Dungeness crab roll, baby back ribs. We chose our favorite foods.

We skipped a wedding cake in favor of a *croquembouche*, a pile of choux pastry balls laced together with caramel or spun sugar in the shape of a tower.

I hadn't heard of this French wedding cake before culinary school, when I had to make one in the traditional tower shape. I loved the idea of it.

Cream puffs, any sort of choux pastry, are my go-to in the sweet cake realm. As a kid I loved éclairs. They're all crispness on the outside, softness on the inside—much more exciting than a traditional cake. And with a croquembouche the couple just tears into it—how fun is that?—as opposed to this formal cake cutting. Brian from Starter Bakery made it. He took some creative license with the size of the balls; they were huge. We kept making bad jokes about it: Huge balls to go with his little buns. Each ball was filled with either passion fruit or vanilla cream. The whole tower was covered in spun sugar, like a deliciously sticky web. It's kind of a messy dessert to eat, which is probably another reason why I loved it.

The day after the wedding celebration—it was Labor Day weekend—we were doing a little post-party cleanup in the backyard. That's when we found a bottle of Roeder champagne in the cooler. Friends had given us the most gorgeous flutes as a wedding present, so at 10:30 in the morning we sat out in our sunny,

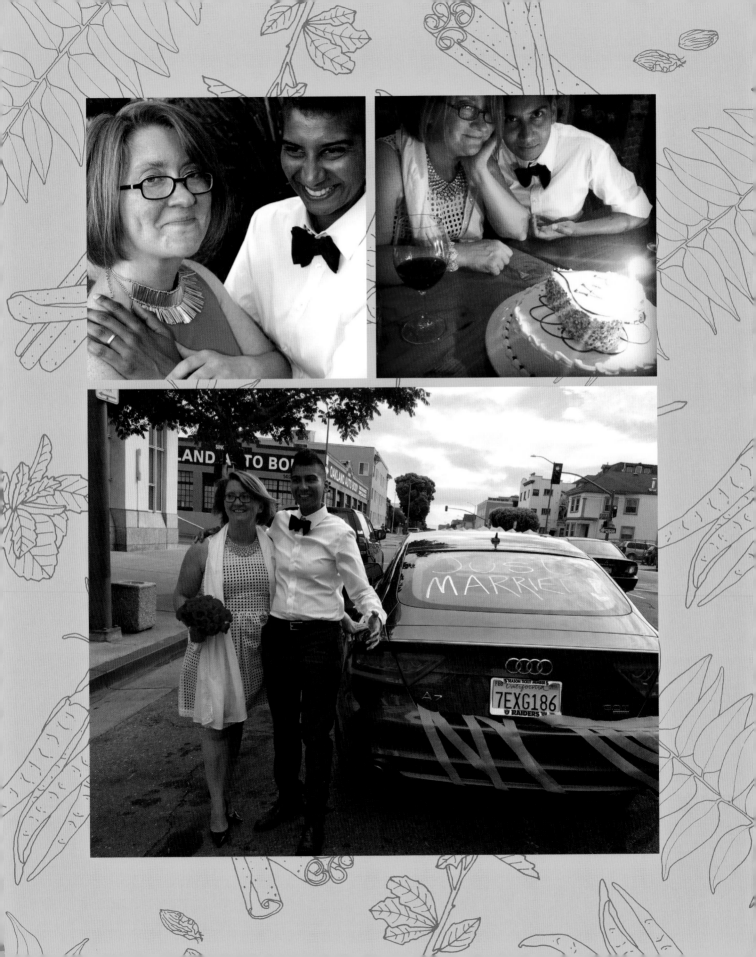

fruit-tree-filled backyard drinking champagne and eating croquembouche in our pajamas. It was the beginning of another very good day.

||||||||||||||||||||||

I identify as American. I also identify as a person of Indian origin. I don't really know India; I'm a tourist there. I've been there at ages five, fifteen, and twice in my thirties. When I was five, from what I understand, I was really into it. When I was fifteen, I was like: "Oh my God, this is so smelly and dirty and I don't want to be here with my parents." As a thirty-something, going to India was intense.

Mumbai is exciting and exhausting. There's the glamour—thriving food culture, modern artsy ambience juxtaposed with grand, fading architectural gems, Bollywood star-spotting. There's also the intense grittiness—the traffic, noise, pollution, crush of humanity, poverty. It's all wrapped up together in one vibrant, colorful package that can leave you on the precipice of sensory overload.

I'm a big-city person, but Mumbai is not like any other city. It's a tough city to navigate as a tourist. Even when I travel with my mother—who is fluent in Hindi, Marathi, Gujarati, and a little Urdu—after thirty-five years of living in the United

States she's no longer a local and doesn't look like one either. Rickshaw rides are fine for short jaunts around town if you have a specific destination, but I've found if you really want to explore the city, hiring a driver to shuttle you between neighborhoods and share insider insights is the way to go.

That's my physical and mental connection to the city. There's also a conflicting emotional push-pull to the place. I feel like I was doubly estranged from India for a big chunk of my life. As a little kid, being from the United States and having other kids making fun of me, I remember wishing I wasn't Indian. I wished I was "normal" like all the other kids. I wanted to distance myself from being Indian. I just wanted to be American. And I didn't go to India between fifteen and thirty so I wouldn't have to explain myself. I'm an unapologetically queer woman, and my parents were not really ready to explain that to my family in India. So I just stayed away instead of pushing them out of their comfort zone or compromising my own truth.

As a teenager, I was probably at the peak of my disdain for being Indian (read: different). I wasn't particularly interested in my surroundings, whether at home or traveling. Now I want to

COOKING AT HOME

I admit it. Since I started cooking professionally—and now that I have two restaurants to run—I don't cook at home nearly as much as I used to or would like. That's a professional hazard. Ask any chef.

But when we do make dinner together, I usually keep it simple: Ann loves pasta. We'll pair a bowl of noodles with seasonal veggies and herbs from the garden. I also find dinner inspiration by poking around in the JBC fridge. I call it shopping at the restaurant: I might grab a bunch of chard, some fingerling potatoes, a few handfuls of salad mix.

Sundays, if I'm not at the restaurant, I might roast a whole chicken on my outdoor rotisserie grill. We're in Northern California, remember, we can grill for nine months of the year or more. I'll make a dry brine with salt, spices, and herbs from the garden, such as oregano and rosemary, as well as lemon zest and a chunk of butter. The best part: sitting in the backyard with a glass of wine while the chicken rotates and develops a crispy brown skin and juicy meat.

Ann's my sous chef in our home kitchen—we've been together so long she anticipates my needs and my movements—she'll cut herbs, prep produce, put things away. We have an easy rapport. And we actually like to sit down at the dining room table—versus balancing a plate on our laps in front of the TV—to have a rare meal together at home as a couple. These days, they're precious.

DIWALI PUDDING

Makes 12 servings

For the pudding:

1 pinch saffron

2 tablespoons whole milk

1 quart Greek yogurt

1 tablespoon green cardamom pods

1½ cup powdered sugar

zest of one lemon

2 cups heavy whipping cream

For the fruit compote:

1 tablespoon neutral oil

1 teaspoon cumin seeds

1 teaspoon nigella seeds

1 tablespoon ginger, minced

2 cups diced seasonal fruit (such as
   strawberries, pears, nectarines,
   gooseberries)

½ teaspoon turmeric powder

½ cup granulated sugar

¼ cup white wine vinegar

Crispy Tikki Puris
   (recipe follows, page 277)

For the garnish:

1 cup pistachios

½ cup powdered sugar (for dusting)

1 cup fresh pomegranate seeds

The impetus for this composed dessert: the Hindu holiday, Diwali. This New Year celebration is also called the Festival of Lights. The JBC Diwali pudding features *shrikhand* and puri, a classic Gujarati combination. Shrikhand is a sweetened yogurt pudding. The traditional puri for this dish is a plain, whole-wheat, pliable bread. I reimagined this dessert combination by lightening the pudding, making a crispy puri, and topping it all with a seasonal fruit compote. The dough for the Crispy Tikki Puris can be made a couple of days ahead, and kept chilled, as can the pudding. This is a special occasion dessert to make for a dinner party.

To make the pudding:

Place the saffron and milk into a small bowl and set it in a warm place for about 10 minutes. Stir to release the saffron flavor into the milk. In a large bowl, mix the saffron milk with the yogurt and stir to fully incorporate ingredients. In a spice grinder, pulse the cardamom pods into a powder. Shake the ground cardamom through a sieve to remove any large pieces. Add the ground cardamom to the yogurt mixture along with the sugar and lemon zest. Whip the cream in a large bowl until stiff peaks form. Fold the cream into the yogurt pudding and chill for at least 2 hours.

To make the fruit compote:

Heat a small saucepan on medium. Add the oil and cumin and nigella seeds. Brown the seeds slightly—about 1 minute. Stir in the ginger, cook for about 2 minutes, and then add the fruit, turmeric, and sugar. The sugar will begin to dissolve; continue to stir for about 3 minutes. Pour in the vinegar, using a spoon to scrape any bits that stick to the bottom of the pan. Lower the heat to medium low and let this simmer until the liquid is reduced by half, about 10 minutes. The time may vary depending on the fruit used. For instance, soft fruits will cook down

(recipe continues)

faster than firm fruits. When the liquid has reduced, chill the compote for at least 30 minutes.

To prep the garnishes:
Preheat the oven to 350°F. Place the pistachios on a sheet pan and toast them in the oven for about 5 to 10 minutes. Remove the pan from the heat and let the pistachios cool. Then roughly chop them.

To assemble the plated dessert:
In a dessert bowl spread a tablespoon of the pudding on the bottom and then place the puri on top. Scoop a large dollop of the pudding and drop the mixture on top of the puri. Drizzle with the fruit compote, dust with the powdered sugar, and garnish with the pomegranate seeds and pistachio.

Crispy Tikki Puris

Makes 10 to 12 puris

1 cup all-purpose flour
   (+¼ cup for dusting)
½ teaspoon salt
1 teaspoon Curry Powder
   (see recipe page 110)
1 tablespoon Ghee (see recipe
   page 22)
6 tablespoons warm water
3 quarts neutral oil (for deep-frying)
¼ cup powdered sugar

Tikki means spicy or savory in Hindi. These crispy puris have a little kick to them, which balances out all the sweet elements in this dessert. We like to dust them with powdered sugar right as they come out of the fryer to seal in the sweetness.

In a mixing bowl combine the flour with the salt and curry powder. Make a well in the center of the dry ingredients and pour in the ghee and warm water. Using a mixer fitted with a dough hook, start mixing the dough on medium speed. The dough will take at least 5 minutes to come together. Turn off the mixer and check the dough's consistency. It should be smooth but not sticky. If the dough is not smooth, add a few drops of water and mix again. If the dough is sticky, add a tablespoon of flour and mix again. When the dough is smooth but not sticky and forms a ball, remove it from the mixer and wrap it in plastic wrap for at least 30 minutes to rest. The dough can chill in plastic wrap for up to 3 days.

Heat the oil in a medium saucepan to 350°F. Use a thermometer to check the temperature. Using a dough cutter, cut off a quarter of the rested dough. Keep all the dough under a moist towel to prevent it from drying out. Roll the cut quarter into a log, about ½-inch thick. Cut into 1-inch long pieces; they will look a little like gnocchi. Press the two cut ends to form a small thick round. Continue doing this with all the dough.

Roll out each portioned dough piece into a thin round, about 5 inches in diameter. Using a small paring knife, make ½-inch-long slits all over the dough. This will keep the dough from puffing up in the frying process. Drop the rolled puris into the hot oil one at a time. Flip the puri over after the first minute to ensure even frying on both sides. Remove the puri after about 3 to 5 minutes, when it is crispy and golden brown on both sides. Dust the puri with powdered sugar and set aside.

Recipe Index

Subject Index

A

Acme Chophouse, 248
amchoor (amchur), 18–19, 100
Amin, Idi, 64, 66
Assil, Reem, 153
authenticity, 218–219, 221

B

balance, 100
Bassin, Sophie, 156–157
Beaver, John, 112
belan, 20
bhaji, 38
Birdsall, John, 251
Bi-Rite, 72
black cardamom pods, 98, 101
Black Lives Matter, 135
black peppercorns, 100
black salt, 19, 100
BlackOUT Collective, 135
blenders, 20
Bon Appétit Management Company (BAMCO),
    244–245, 248
Borba Farms, 154
Bourdain, Anthony, 199, 251
bread, types of, 218
Brown, Michael, 135
brunch service, 219–221
butter, 14

C

candy thermometer, 20
cardamom, 98, 101
cassava, 63
cassia, 98, 100
chaat, 112
Chai Pani Restaurant Group, 217
Charlie's Cafe, 248
chickpea flour, 16
chickpeas/chana, 14
chile de árbol, 100
chiles, 16–17, 100
chili powder, 19, 100
Choi, Roy, 119
cholle bhature, 112

Chopra, Amod, 112
cinnamon, 100
Claridge's Hotel, 246–247
cloves, 100
coconut milk, 14
coconuts, 31
Colicchio, Tom, 243–244
comfort food, 63–64, 66–71
Cook and Her Farmer, The, 150
cooking at home, 271
Cooking Project, 118–119
coriander seeds, 98
Cosecha, 150
croquembouche, 268, 270
culinary school, 245–246
Cullors, Patrisse, 135
cumin, 98
curry, 190
curry leaves, 17

D

dal, 14
"day in the life," 178–185
de Young Museum, 248
Dinwoodie, Aaron, 156
Dirty Girl Produce, 154–155
diversity, 115–116, 120–121, 184, 223, 247–248

E

Edible Excursions, 198–199
Elco Pani Puri Centre, 32

F

Fahrer, Benjamin, 162, 181
failure, 243–244, 247
farms and farmers' markets, 149–150,
    153–157, 162
fenugreek, 98
fenugreek leaves, 17
Feral Heart Farm, 156–157
Festival of Colors/Sharing Love, 228
fondue, 72–73
food mill, 20
Food Network, 217
food tours, 198–199
Full Belly Farm, 154
"fusion" label, 217, 219

ACKNOWLEDGMENTS

It turns out writing a book is a lot like running a restaurant. It's not something you can do alone. It takes a team.

I'd like to thank key members of my team for their love, support, talent, skills, and guidance—and for covering nights on the line when I was at work on these pages.

To begin at the beginning: A big shout out to Mom & Dad (Bhagwati and Dr. Arvindkumar Mistry) for making me, loving me, feeding me, educating me, providing a solid foundation from which I could launch, and supporting my decision to open my own restaurant in a funky little corner of Oakland. You are my biggest fans.

Shout out to my whole family: both Ba and Dadaji, my many Kakas and Kakis, Fois and Fuas, Mama and Mami, Masa and Masi, *so* many cousins, and my sisters for their mutual affection and for gathering together in a kitchen and around a table. Their love of food, drink, and family feasts has been ingrained in me since birth.

Thank you to my wife's parents, Jim and Marie Nadeau, for, well, making her of course. Also, for your continued cheerleading and practical "roll up your sleeves" work. Your hard work in helping to transform this space—from sanding tables to cleaning out all the random crap we found—was so appreciated.

To my early culinary mentors—I'm talking about you Chef David Selex, Chef Julio Flames, Fedele Bauccio, Amarylla Ganner, and Chef Thom Fox—thanks for teaching me, believing in me, and nurturing me in an industry where those traits can be in short supply.

To the food writers who "get" me and championed the restaurant early on—that includes you John Birdsall, Kerry Diamond, and Luke Tsai—thanks so much for the support. Thanks to John, Kerry, and Anthony Bourdain for the book blurbs that appear on this cover. I truly appreciate the kind, thoughtful words.

To Chef Tanya Holland and Chef Dominica Rice-Cisneros, two talented women in Oakland's restaurant culture, fist bumps for support and solidarity. Ditto to Brian Wood of Starter Bakery, my buddy in food business matters, who also makes terrific baked goods.

To the JBC cookbook crew in the San Francisco Bay Area: I literally couldn't have done this without you. Props to agent Danielle Svetcov for seeing the potential here and for help navigating bookland. Love to photographer Alanna Hale, food stylist Ethel Brennen, and photography assistant Nicola Parisi for making shoot days such a blast, even when your attention to detail almost did me in. It was totally worth it: the gorgeous images that grace these pages capture the spirit and soul of JBC. Hugs, as well, to Iris Gottlieb for her awesome, whimsical illustrations that pop up throughout this book.

To my co-writer, friend, and fellow immigrant Sarah Henry: Thanks for your storytelling chops in these chapters, for showcasing both me and my restaurant in articles early on, and for embracing the role of taskmaster with humor, even when you learned I was launching a second restaurant while we were writing this book. Thank you for being a good listener, your endless curiosity, and for helping draw out the kinds of details that transform a series of disparate stories into a cohesive book.

To the JBC cookbook team at Running Press: Thanks for valuing what I wanted to say in these pages, while also being excited about the restaurant and its recipes, and for collaborating on this cookbook/memoir from the beginning. You took the raw ingredients and turned it into a beautiful book. High fives to editor Shannon Connors, designer Jason Kayser, and copy editor Ashley Benning

for your professionalism and enthusiasm for this project from start to finish.

To Munira Lokhandwala, cookbook recipe coordinator, big thanks for your organization skills and support on that end. Thanks as well to my trusty recipe testers for your frank and fast feedback: Haven Bourque, Ashley Chavez, Amarylla Ganner, Randi Gerson, Gretchen Grathwohl, Hannah Horovitz, Lisa Rogovin, Dana Rosenberg, Rebecca Sibrack, Elitsa Somleva, and Dipti Vyas.

To my JBC regular diners: Thanks for supporting a small, mom-and-mom owned restaurant and eating with us on a routine basis. Our customers are also our community. Juhu's menu would not be possible without the many local farmers who share their pristine produce with us. Special nod to hyperlocal growers Sophie Bassin and Aaron Dindwoodie of Feral Heart Farm, Benjamin Fahrer of Top Leaf Farms, and Marsha Habib of Oya Organics.

To staff both current and former: There wouldn't be a Juhu Beach Club cookbook if not for you all. Singling out here Melissa Smith, my ubertalented, badass chef de cuisine, whose positivity, calm, and leadership in the kitchen is priceless. Melissa's palate, work ethic, and playfulness makes her

a great fit at JBC. Thanks for holding down the fort at the mothership during both the birth of this book and our sister location Navi Kitchen.

To the JBC back and front of house staff who make it possible to open our doors every day, my heartfelt thanks and gratitude to all you bring to the table. That list of employees includes Suchi Amin, Moises Aquino, Sophie Bassin, Armando Bibiano, Jessica Castro, James Cox, Emily Fowler, Cara Greene, Ayele Hadiya, Shelley Harrison, Jhe N'earo Hemingway, Hannah Horovitz, Olivia Lee, Samuel Littlefield, Andres Lopez, Jasmine Lyons, Teddy Newport, Kathryn Novotny, Sissy Silva, Emmanuel Singh, Gilberto Suastegui, Drew Wilder, and Alek Zito.

Special mention must be made of David Bush, a talented, young line cook who worked at JBC on and off for three years. I appreciated his quiet focus next to me in the kitchen. He left us too soon. Much love to his mother and father, Carolyn Yale and Rock Bush, for their continued support in the face of great loss.

I'd be remiss if I didn't give a shout out to some of our newbies at JBC and Navi, already showing up like fam in a short space of time: Wafa Aouadj, Hajera Ghori , Sajo Jefferson, Nikki Lazio, Britni Mills, Valerie Perez Ordonez, Phoebe Sanders, Golda Sargento, and Orly Zamir.

To my chosen family who have eaten at our dinner table, stopped by my pop up, and supported JBC in so many different ways, I heart you all. You have helped keep me grounded during all the highs and lows over the years. Hugs and kisses to Gretchen Gathwohl and Geeta Makhija, their kids Naveen and Leela; Randi Gerson and Sara Lesser, their kids Matteo and Eden; and Micia Mosely and Jilchristina Vest. And much love to our dear friends, the "Super Seniors,"

Elizabeth Ann and Milton Moskowitz. Thank you to good friends and early supporters of the JBC pop-up, Linda Palermo, Lori Lincoln, and Paul Young.

A gigantic thank you to Lynn Larosa for keeping our insane restaurant books in order and advising us with a stoic sensibility.

Saving the best for last, to my wife Ann Nadeau, my partner in work and life, look what we've created together, honey. I wouldn't be here without your love, support, loyalty, cheerleading, and unflinching belief in my abilities as a chef, restaurant owner, and human being.

Thank you for moving with me to San Francisco on a whim, encouraging me to attend culinary school in London, suggesting I pop up at a sketchy liquor store in San Francisco, and helping find a home for us in Oakland. Thanks, too, for making the interior of Juhu such a warm and welcoming space, washing dishes at 1 in the morning, printing menus, sourcing cool plates, attending restaurant supply auctions, and reminding me when to say yes and when to say no. And, of course, thank you for exploring India with me, agreeing to marry me, and being the person I want to go home to every night.

Thanks for your support, patience, and suggestions in the creation of this book, too.

Most of all, thanks for loving me, all of me, in all my complicated glory.

Making dinner for you, just the two of us, is one of my greatest joys.